It's All About Her
Bringing Back Chivalry for the 21st Century Guy

It's All About Her
Bringing Back Chivalry for the 21st Century Guy

Written By: Lance Ranzer
with
Adam Choit

Published in the United States

Library of Congress Cataloging-in-Publication Data
Ranzer, Lance.
It's All About Her:
Bringing Back Chivalry for the 21st Century Guy

Website: www.itsallaboutherthebook.com
Twitter: @AllAboutHerBook

ISBN 978-0-9913336-3-9987-0-9913336-3-9

Printed in the United States of America

First Edition

Acknowledgments:

Writing a book can often be an individual project, but the reality is that without the friends and family with me through the past thirty years of my life, I would not have been able to make this a reality.

I'd first like to thank my parents, Ruth and Martin, as well as my sisters, Llanie, Sharon, and Erica, my beautiful niece Talan, and nephews Brandon and Tatem. Next, a huge thanks to all my friends, family members, and ex-girlfriends, who have all touched me at some point in my life. You all have in some way, shape, or form, taught me how to become a better person and to build confidence, and more importantly, to never give up.

To Kailee Loughlin, my copy editor. Thank you for your amazing grammar and language skills. You have helped the book get to the next step, and for this I am grateful.

Finally, to Adam Choit, my ghostwriter. Thank you for your wisdom, your patience, the many hours you have spent working with me, "going to Jackson," but most importantly, believing in this book and me. Your dedication and willingness to see this through 'til the end shows what an incredible collaborator and friend you truly are!

Table of Contents

Introduction

Well, you've made the decision to purchase my book. I'm not sure where you made this transaction, but perhaps while strolling through the aisles of your local bookstore, something about this particular item caught your eye. Or, perhaps you heard about this book on the Internet or by word of mouth.

Whether you're male or female, I guarantee that you will get your money's worth here. While this book is more intended for guys, girls can also benefit. Hopefully, girls reading this can grasp a better understanding of what guys go through in life in order to meet a very special girl like yourself. Listen, not every guy is born with the ability to instinctively know to match the color of a belt with the color of his shoes, but yes, it is possible to learn this, and you may soon laugh at how obvious and essential such simple tasks are to complete.

This book is not a "guaranteed to get laid" guide. Nor by reading this book will you automatically have success in relationships. But, the following information contains suggestions and clear examples of how young men can improve their self-confidence, self-esteem, and mental and/or physical well-being. In addition, ways to better your social, sexual, and personal relationships will be examined.

Many of you guys out there might already have certain philosophies and routines that work very well for you. That's great. If something's working for you, stick with it. If you feel like you are content in your life in terms of your relationships with women, keep doing what you're doing. I'm not trying to change or mold people into an image of myself. My goal is to reach out to the average guy who's seeking help and advice. Even if you think you have it all together, I bet that you'll find plenty of useful tidbits that you'll appreciate.

The target audience for this book is something that I've thought long and hard about. The demographic that I'd like to reach is a wide range of young men between the ages of eighteen and forty years old. But more importantly than age, I'm specifically aiming for those who are good and genuine individuals, with noble intentions. I'm also seeking out those who are hard-working professionals. With that being said, what I'm about to share can also strike a chord with blue-collar types, just as much as with those who work in a more white-collar environment. The common thread is that I want to help guys who may lack certain tools, skills, or even physical attributes, but who still want to find love and happiness.

By no means am I a doctor or a physician, nor do I believe that I have all the answers. But, I would like to tell you a little bit about who I am, and what inspired me to share some of my personal experiences and insights.

For legal reasons, some names have been changed and some places are undefined. No individual story is a personal attack on anyone, anything, or even on myself, for that matter. For my friends, exes, family members, or anybody else who I may have missed, please take this book with a grain of salt. All the girls from my life who are mentioned should read on with a sense of humor, and even a sense of pride and accomplishment, because it is you who helped shape me to become a better person over the years. You've given me the confidence and ability to write this book in the first place. It is the treasured experiences with you that made me realize that guys can learn an awful lot from women, and no guy should ever think that he knows everything.

* * *

My name is Lance Ranzer. I live in Los Angeles, California, and I work as a visual effects artist in the film industry. I think that it's important for everyone to have interests, hobbies, and passions in life. I joined the football team in the sixth grade and played through my senior year in high school. I loved the game, but let's be honest, if you're not a 6'5", 250-pound genetic freak who runs like lightning, it's tough to continue a football career beyond high school. Since I don't play football anymore, I've taken to other interests, such as sky diving, scuba diving, and I've even gone cliff jumping. I love traveling the world, I enjoy the beauty of the outdoors, and I try to appreciate what life has to offer as much as I can. In addition to what I've already mentioned, I also enjoy all sorts of other athletic activities, such as hiking, running, and rock climbing. A lot of this might sound a little like living on the edge, but hey, as far as I know, you only live once.

I'm in my early 30's and would like to think of myself as a good-hearted, old-school type of guy. I'm not perfect, but I am a proud individual who has enjoyed and appreciated some of the benefits in life that have not always come so easily. I've definitely paid a lot of dues to get where I am today.

Anyway, I transferred to the University of Central Florida (UCF) as a sophomore, coming from Valencia

Community College with an Associate in Arts Degree. I was lucky enough to have already figured out my career goals as an aspiring visual effects artist. I believed that UCF provided the best opportunity to study in my desired field.

When I transferred to UCF, I never thought that I would have any interest in joining a fraternity. By college standards, I felt like I was too old to pledge, since I was already twenty-one and in my junior year. My roommate, whom I did not know before enrolling, happened to already be a brother of the fraternity that would soon become a crucial part of my life. I look back on my fraternity days with nothing but fond memories. In fact, I consider this time of my life to be an essential phase that contributed immeasurably to my development as a person. "I am a fraternity guy, not for a day, week, or month -- but for life." This is a quote that I first heard maybe ten years ago, but for me, it has served as a mantra, and it is a significant part of my foundation as a person. I always encourage college students to get involved with the Greek system. If you don't feel likea fraternity is for you, participate in social activities, clubs, and organizations connected with your school. The more involved you are, the more opportunity there is to meet girls!

Many people have certain associations with fraternity brothers, or "frat boys," but I feel like it is essential to know the kind of person somebody is before you group them in any kind of stereotype. Many people skeptically accuse fraternities to be nothing more than a place to "buy friends." I assure you that this definitely doesn't apply to every single fraternity and sorority. Just because someone wears letters on their chest doesn't

mean that they paid for their friends or that they shoul be
unfairly placed into some sort of category. I felt a
powerful connection to my brothers, and I will feel this
way for the rest of my life.

I first heard about open houses when I was a
sophomore in college. Fraternity houses opened their
doors to welcome all types of guys. More importantly,
sorority girls were also present at these events, sporting
that particular frat's letters. I visited about a dozen
houses, but eventually decided to pledge the one where I
felt the most comfortable. The reason was quite simple --
I connected the most with this particular group of guys
(A.E.K.D.B.), and it didn't hurt that a lot of their
attractive female friends hung out at the house. I did
realize that some of the girls were just for show, and that
they were helping out the house by meeting and greeting
potential pledges. However, a lot of these girls were
connected and knew the best places to party. At the time,
as a young college student, this was key to me.

I always felt safe and comfortable around my
brothers. Trust was never an issue amongst the guys. I
felt this way as soon as I unpacked my belongings and
settled into my room in this enormous and imposing
structure that would be my residence for the next couple
of years. I remember that the fraternity house seemed like
a hotel. Moreover, it was a place where I was going to
live with good friends, who would all eventually become
true brothers, who I never had growing up, and always
wanted.

Another highly significant part of my development
as a young man was the fact that I did grow up with two
older sisters. My sister Llanie, the middle child, had (and
still has) the devastating combination of both brains and

looks. She was able to go party, and then the next day take a midterm and still score at the top of her class. She also played on the soccer and softball teams. Always with the popular crowd, Llanie attracted the cool and good-looking guys.

She always had girlfriends over for sleepovers, and I often tried to make conversation with these very welcome guests. At the time, I felt like my sister's friends were far out of my league. I could only fantasize about them paying any attention to me. The best that I could do was to literally keep my door open, eavesdrop on their conversations, and retain as much from "girl talk" as I could. Some of the time, well, let's be honest, most of the time what they talked about was boring girl stuff. However, they spoke a bit about their relationships with guys, thus making my listening well worth my time. I definitely reaped benefits from these conversations. I recall them talking about "cool people," but more importantly, I learned about the importance of becoming friends with the "up and coming" cool people, so one day I would be on the same "level" of girls my sister brought by when I was a freshman in high school.

My oldest sister Sharon was 5'0", 95 pounds, but could take on senior varsity football players face to face and easily humble them. Back then, middle and high school kids rode the bus together. I was only in sixth grade, and a 300-pound varsity lineman was pushing me around. It wasn't until this courageous girl made me realize that, although it might be a cliché, "It's not the size of the dog in the fight, it's the size of the fight in the dog." I followed her lead and learned how to stick up for myself.

One phrase that many of us have heard in our lives

while riding home on the bus is: "You're in my seat! Get the fuck up!" One time, I heard these words when a bully suddenly snatched my books from my hands. At first, I stood up and went to grab them back, but just as I did, my belongings were launched toward the front of the bus. This prick laughed, pushed me out of the way, and then sat down in my seat, high-fiving his surrounding friends. Embarrassed, I went to retrieve my books, as others stared. Needless to say, all of the cute girls watched as well, thus eliminating any shot with them.

That's when Sharon stepped in and got involved. She yelled, and her saliva launched into this lineman's face. She wagged her finger right in his grill. "You better go pick my brother's books up and let him sit where he damn well pleases, before I beat the living shit out of you. Don't fuck with me right now!" This huge bully turned pale white as he was put in his place. This is when I realized that I could stand up for myself. At that moment, I learned the value of speaking up and the importance of defending myself. I knew that I needed to apply this mentality to all areas of my life in the future. Even to this day, I remember this as a turning point for me. Thank you, big sister.

I also want to give a shout-out to both my mother and father, who always did their very best to teach me good manners and a respect for people and for life. Of course, by no means did I agree with everything they did while raising me, but looking back now, I think that they did a pretty fantastic job, and for this I'm forever grateful. My mother always emphasized the importance of politeness, and that the simple "pleases" and "thank yous" go a long way. Every mother tells their child to treat others how s/he would like to be treated. This message was always at the forefront of the lessons that my mother passed down to me.

I always looked up to, and admired my father's dedicated work ethic. He constantly reinforced that what you put into life is what you get out, and that nothing comes free and easy. He taught me the value of doing things yourself. He instilled in me the idea that I shouldn't rely on others all the time. Through this lesson, I was able to experience and appreciate the joy that comes from a sense of accomplishment.

Having said this, there's only so much one can learn from listening and observing friends and family. There comes a point when a man has to walk to the edge of the cliff, jump off, and then build his wings on the way down. There's only so much knowledge and wisdom that can be passed along from person to person. The rest must be discovered through personal experiences and trial and error.

This honest and from-the-heart text is part "how to" and part "biography." I don't want this book to be merely words on paper, and I don't want to be just a random person talking to you. I really want to be closer than that, more along the lines of a trustworthy friend, who you'd swear you've known since adolescence. I want to be someone who you feel like you can rely on for sound advice.

Guys, I know you are eager to read some juicy stuff about how to deal with the opposite sex, but before you even set foot out the door to meet girls, there should be a reasonable amount of thought that goes into your preparation. This consists of varying aspects of your life, which will be examined shortly. You can't expect to go from strike-out to homerun overnight by thinking that girls are going to come to you just because you think that you're God's gift to the universe. Some devotion to personal improvement is an absolute essential for every guy out there!

Chapter 1: Home & Car Maintenance

Hey guys, when was the last time you had your car washed? When's the last time you had the interior vacuumed and cleaned? Do you even know what having your car detailed means? If the answers to these questions are mostly, "I have no idea," then this is one of the very first things you want to take care of before you pick up a girl for something like a first date.

Regardless of what you drive, you want to take just as much pride in your car as you would with the home in which you live. There is no excuse for having candy wrappers on the floor or empty bottles lying around. Before entering the car wash, thoroughly dispose of all garbage or any other loose items that you don't need. This should be done <u>before</u> the interior is vacuumed.

If you opt not to have the interior cleaned at the car wash, or the place doesn't do interiors, there are other options. Many car wash facilities have vacuums available for customer use. Also, many gas stations have vacuums that you can use that cost no more than a couple of bucks. In addition, if you happen to own a portable vacuum, go ahead and use it before you head through the car wash.

Most car washes will include a vacuum, an "Armorall" of your interior, and they might even check the air pressure in your tires. Be shrewd with your money, but also take advantage of the services available to you. Since you only need to wash the vehicle every few weeks (or on an as needed basis), this is a good opportunity for you to check the pressure in your tires. At most car washes, they usually spray the interior with an air freshener to give it that clean, new car smell, but if not, please, please, please do not purchase and hang a taxicab air freshener from your rearview mirror. This is tacky. Your vehicle might not actually smell like a urinal, but these air fresheners are used in dingy gas station restrooms, reminding others riding with you of such places. What you'll want to purchase is a flavored spray or incense can. These products are available at any auto parts store, or at places like Target in the automotive section. A good place to store a deodorizer like this is under the driver's seat.

Have a stash of napkins in the glove box for times when you sneeze, have minor spills, or for when a girl does her makeup. Always make sure that when you go out on a date, you have a full tank of gas. You never know when she might lean over and take a look at the gas gauge. This may sound silly, but it's a nice little detail for a girl when you're out with her. It will make her feel that much more secure with you. Believe me, she's most likely looking at you, and wondering, "Could I see myself and this guy in a relationship?" These little details that she may or may not pick up on can't hurt, and will only help you have a more successful date.

It's always a good idea to have some emergency cash stashed somewhere in your automobile. God forbid that your car breaks down at an inopportune time; you can always pay for a taxi to get your girl home safely. Any amount between $40 and $60 is wise. Split it up into $20's, $10's, $5's, and dollar bills. Always have some quarters and other change in your car as well. Believe it or not, change is very useful. Who knows when you might need to pay for parking or a toll? One day you will thank me for this tidbit of advice.

So while you're out getting your car vacuumed, cleaned, and washed, this is the perfect time to stock up on the essentials for you and your home. Bathroom cleanliness should be important to everyone, but guys often neglect this responsibility and it can make or break your chances with a girl.

There are a few basic necessities when it comes to maintaining a well-kept bathroom. One is remembering to squeegee the shower doors regularly -- that means after every use. It probably takes under 15 seconds to do. If you have curtains instead of a door, spray the curtains with Comet, in addition to the tub and the walls, then rinse. You'll find that many of these products don't even require scrubbing or rinsing. Spray on, and you're done. Next time that you're at the supermarket, try reading a few labels. You might be pleasantly surprised with what you learn.

Keeping your shower clean is not a difficult task. All it takes is Comet, a Brillo pad, and a little elbow grease. Comet and Brillo pads are inexpensive items available almost anywhere, such as your local supermarket, Target, or even at the dollar store. Just like your toilet, look at the surface of your shower closely to see if it's clean. What I mean by clean is: clean enough for a girl to not mind getting on her knees for you. Yeah, I said it!

A girl does not want to sit on or be near any strange hair, dried-up urine, or shit-splatter. Not to mention the disgusting iron rim around the inside of your toilet bowl -- it's a clear indicator of the last time you cleaned it, which was much too long ago. It's as easy as this -- some Comet, along with a toilet brush used in a simple twirling motion. Go back and forth to cover all areas of the bowl. Do this until the stained rim is gone and your toilet returns to its natural color. Be sure to look and see that it's gone. Don't assume that a couple of swirls around the bowl removed all the nastiness off your toilet. Proceed to spray underneath and on the toilet seat, using a Lysol spray can. Next, grab some toilet paper and wipe the area down until all the urine, hair, and other grime is completely gone.

My next big question to you is: how many rolls of toilet paper do you have in your bathroom? Not outside, but in the actual bathroom itself. If the answer isn't at least two (one new roll and one in use), what's going to happen when you bring a girl back to your place for the first time and she doesn't realize she needs more paper until after the fact? This could embarrass her by making her feel awkward in asking for a roll. Be sure to have a roll on the spool at all times, and an extra one visible either on a shelf or in plain sight once your cabinet is opened. Remember, if you don't have a shelf, inside a cabinet would be the next place somebody would look.

When a girl innocently opens your bathroom cabinet looking for something like a fresh roll of toilet paper, you want her to see that you take care of your belongings. It's worth noting that you should keep all of your bathroom cabinets and drawers neat and organized, not just for your own purposes, but for occasions like the ones that I'm discussing. It can only score you extra brownie points with her when she sees that you pay attention to keeping areas clean that aren't even in plain sight, such as the inside of a bathroom cabinet. The best way to avoid guests going through your cabinets unnecessarily is to keep your bathroom fully stocked and presentable with a few basic items. This is especially important to do before you go out on a date.

Also, you shouldn't set a roll of toilet paper on the floor. It is likely to get wet or ruined. Every single item you own must have a place where it belongs. When girls enter a guy's home for the first time, they immediately sense whether or not the guy is organized. They can sense if a guy cares about his personal belongings. When a girl considers dating you, being clean is an easy way to give her some reassurance.

As far as bathroom garbage cans are concerned, it is expected that some frightening items will find their way inside them. That being said, you don't have to keep your trash can empty at all times. Having some trash in the can is not a problem, but when you are going out on a date or expecting company, empty out your shaved pubic trimmings, wads of other mysterious hair, and those dirty Q-tips. Don't assume that she won't peek in there. Trust me, she will. Don't be alarmed by this behavior, just be prepared for it. It means that she's possibly interested in you!

It's a bad situation when you clog up your own toilet, but just imagine what it might be like should she clog up the toilet, and even worse, there isn't a plunger handy! If she's forced into a situation where she needs to call you into the bathroom for help, your odds of having another date with this girl are greatly diminished. As embarrassing as it might be for her to ask you for toilet paper, asking for a plunger is 1000 times more humiliating. The bottom line is that you should own a plunger. Keep it under the sink in the cabinet, or behind or next to the toilet.

It doesn't take that much time to complete the

simple and very manageable tasks that I've discussed. If it's clear that you take the time for upkeep, guests in your home will feel comfortable and relaxed around you. Isn't that what you want? Most people don't want to spend any time in a stinky and dirty bathroom. A filthy bathroom reflects on how you take care of yourself. I honestly believe that it's important to take pride in your stuff, especially anything that you've worked hard to purchase.

Here are some more bathroom tips in terms of items that you should always have. First of all, have liquid soap next to your sink. It's not the end of the world if you have bar soap there, but liquid soap is more efficient and just looks a little classier. A bar of soap is usually intended for the shower, whereas liquid soap is better for just washing one's hands and face.

Have at least one candle or incense on the counter. Also, it's a wise idea to have matches readily available, not only to light your candles, but striking a match is a quick way to deal with unwanted odors. Although I prefer candles and incense, a simple spray air freshener is efficient too. Make sure to have a clean towel hanging on a hook or rack that's ready and available for use. Paper towels on a rack or spool work nicely as well. Guests should always have something to dry their hands with, on something other than your main bath towel.

Even before a girl sees your bathroom, she will usually pass through the kitchen area. Not to be sexist (and this isn't always the case), but typically, girls know more about kitchens than the average guy. She'll spot that pile of dishes the second she enters the kitchen. A pile of dishes will make her think that you're unorganized and just plain messy. It's not that difficult to do the dishes. Having a clean kitchen is just one more way to show her that you took the time to make your place presentable and that you really do care about this date.

Remember to keep the countertops clean too. Use a paper towel and some Windex and you will be done in a matter of seconds. You may think that Windex is just for glass, but it works just fine on your countertops. It's also a good idea to have some candles on your clean kitchen table. Of all the money that I've spent on incense, sprays, candles, and potpourri, I've come to the conclusion that the best bang for my buck has been to purchase inexpensive scented oils. I recommend using home fragrance oils that are available at stores like Bath & Body Works. Put three or four drops inside a ceramic dish that's placed above a lit tea candle and voila! -- hours of fresh-scented air.

After you take care of the countertops, walk over to the kitchen table and apply Windex to the surface. If you know company is on the way, it's polite to remove any stacks of papers, bills, or other junk that might get in the way of a romantic dinner. Even when you might just be sitting at the table having a casual conversation with somebody, it makes you look unorganized. Plus, why risk spilling a glass of wine or hot candle wax on your bills or other important documents?

If you're going to follow one piece of advice that I've offered you to this point, you should always remember that your refrigerator is not a science experiment. Throw out expired items, and definitely get rid of anything that has turned strange colors. Don't let food get moldy. If you're unsure about something, give the item a quick smell. Don't ever hesitate to throw out any expired perishables. A day or two after the expiration might be okay, but that's it, guys. Here's another good tip: put a small box of baking soda in your fridge and in your freezer. This will keep your fridge smelling fresh.

In your refrigerator, there's a very important item that you should always stock up on -- bottled water. Think about it -- why give a girl tap water from your disgusting and contaminated faucet? Wouldn't you rather just hand her a fresh bottle of water? Plus, after those long nights with her (wink wink), you'll want to re-hydrate with a cool-tasting, non-toxic bottle of natural and purified water. Don't forget that when a girl eventually exits your apartment, it's always a nice gesture to give her a bottle as she leaves. It's a courtesy and a thoughtful parting gift.

As in the bathroom, it's okay to have some garbage in the kitchen trash can, but when you're aware that guests are on their way, take out the trash and put a fresh bag inside. It doesn't hurt to spray the can down with Febreeze too! Here's a simple way to keep the kitchen floor clean: all you need is a broom and a dustpan. If you spot something sticky on the floor, just grab a sponge, add a little soap, and take care of it. I want to mention a very useful product that I recently started using called the Swiffer Sweeper. Don't be afraid to Google this or any other product that I've mentioned that you are unfamiliar with. This product works best on any tile, wood, vinyl, or linoleum floor. It easily picks up dirt in the cloth and makes cleaning a breeze. If you have large areas of hardwood flooring in your home, I suggest trying out the Swiffer Sweeper, but if you're more comfortable with a traditional mop and bucket, there's nothing wrong with choosing that, as long as you're using the appropriate cleaning substances and the job gets done.

For those of you who have carpets, you should own a working vacuum cleaner. It may cost you more than you'd like to spend, but it's an essential item that you'll use regularly. It will pay for itself in a short period of time. Get a vacuum cleaner that comes with an attachable hose to get to the corners and edges of rooms. This should be a bi-weekly activity. I'm not saying that your carpet has to be spotless all the time, nor must you always take off your shoes upon entry, but it is nice to keep it reasonably clean and presentable for that lucky night, when passions are running high and you and your girl return home, but are unable to make it to the bedroom in time! I strongly recommend that if you live in a home with newer carpeting that you go with a "shoes-off policy." This will help preserve the lifespan of the carpet. Also, while we're on the subject, upon entry into someone else's home (especially a girl's), always ask if you should take off your shoes.

For stains on your carpet, Dissolve is a very handy spray stain remover that you should own. Accidents happen all the time, whether it is dirt tracked in or spilled drinks. Using Dissolve or a similar product will help minimize, if not completely eliminate, major stains or damages.

There's also something else that is very useful: carpet and room odor eliminator. It comes in powdered form and is sprinkled lightly throughout carpeted areas. After you've sprinkled the necessary amount, vacuum it up. This will help remove visible powder, and by running your vacuum over it, it will push the excess odor eliminator deeper into the carpet. This will eliminate unpleasant odors in the room, giving it a clean scent. It also kills bacteria that live in your carpet. Using this powder about once a month should make a considerable difference. Keep in mind that it typically takes two to three hours before the odor of the powder subsides. Therefore, if you're expecting company, don't throw powder everywhere ten minutes before expected guests arrive.

* * *

Speaking of making a room look clean and smelling pleasant, wash your bed sheets at least every other week. During the week, spray down your bed with Febreeze or a spray that isn't chemical-based. This will keep your sheets and blankets smelling fresh. It's important that you own at least two sets of blankets, bed sheets and pillowcases. Besides having a spare set ready to go when you're doing a wash, you'd be surprised how much changing your bed sheets can give your entire room a fresh new look. It's also wise to get into the habit of making your bed every morning before you go to work. Not only does routinely making your bed show that you're tidy, but it also lets her know that you appreciate what you've worked hard for.

There are certain items that you should keep by your bed. Be sure to keep condoms close by in a drawer. If you're not that experienced with purchasing protection, my suggestion is to buy any lubricated latex condom. I recommend avoiding un-lubricated condoms. Trust me, there's a huge difference. Un-lubricated condoms aren't as pleasurable and could cause pain or discomfort for both you and her. For the record, condoms do have an expiration date, so if it's been a while, discard the old ones and purchase new ones.

In addition to keeping condoms nearby, it's also not a bad idea to keep a box of tissues and a small hand towel within reach. You never know when you'll have to wipe up "unexpected liquids." Gum or mints nearby can be of good use too.

I have a few more quick tips to pass along to you before we move on to the next chapter:

* Don't leave dirty clothes scattered all over any room or on the floor. If it's dirty, throw it in the hamper. If it's clean, hang it up or fold it neatly into a drawer.
* Don't let the trash can overflow with garbage. Take care of this before it gets to that point.
* Own and use a dust brush for your blinds and computer equipment. Don't forget to dust the furniture and your CDs and DVDs.

Overall, make sure that you keep your living space reasonably neat. You don't need to maintain a pristine home. I'm just suggesting that you keep everything somewhat tidy, especially because you never know when unexpected visitors might pop in, whether it's family, friends, or neighbors. And guys, you never know when your neighbor is going to bring over that hot friend you've been dying to meet!

Chapter 2: Personal Maintenance

As important as it is to take care of your home, car, and other possessions, taking care of yourself is even more crucial. When you're surrounded by people, they can see you. They can smell you. They see how you dress and what you wear, and they can tell whether or not you are a clean person. Of course, it's not always about what other people think, but you should still take pride in how you present yourself to the world. Everyone isn't going to be attracted to your overall presentation, but as long as you put in a sufficient amount of effort, you should feel good about yourself. This will help raise your self-esteem and increase your confidence. We all have doubts, so if you're not the most confident person in the world right now, it's okay. I believe that we can all get to a place where we can feel good about ourselves...at least most of the time.

* * *

Let me begin by naming a few more basic items that you'll need in your bathroom. Keep a bottle of mouthwash in your bathroom cabinet. When you return home from a date, it's a quick and easy breath saver. Nothing is worse than bad breath. Mouthwash is especially useful for quick fixes in the morning, but it's handy for any occasion. You can even gargle some while you're using the John, then jump back into bed with your girl, with newly fresh breath.

Another item you should own is deodorant. You

should always use it. For a few extra bucks, it doesn't hurt to have a back-up either. Guys: do not apply deodorant before you put your shirt on, only after. If you put deodorant on first, in the process of putting your shirt on, it's likely that your shirt will rub against your armpit, causing unwanted, visible deodorant marks, and you don't want residue on your clothing. To properly apply deodorant, grab the front of your shirt and leave enough room for your hand to reach under your shirt to apply the deodorant. Do this without making contact with the garment. Another note is that you don't need to take the deodorant stick and go up and down the ribcage and as far up as your elbow. Finally, if you use a white stick, be especially careful with darker colored shirts, which can stain easily.

Another tip for personal improvement is to use hair wax rather than gel. Fiber, dry wax, or similar products work well. Gel, on the other hand, leaves residue and can give the impression that you have a head full of dandruff. You don't want your shoulders to be covered with flakes. I might also add that no self-respecting guy uses mousse or hairspray. You are not a chick, and we're not in the 1980's anymore. Wax might cost you a few extra bucks, but believe me, it's worth shelling out the money. Girls care very much about their appearance, and you should about yours.

Personal grooming is something that you should have learned by now. It should be part of your everyday routine. It's surprising to me, though, how many guys *don't* practice proper hygiene habits. I've learned over the years that girls care very much about hygiene -- and not just their own, yours too!

It's wise to own tweezers, electric hair clippers,

and of course, nail clippers. Tweezers, perhaps a girlie object or something foreign to you, are actually useful to remove unsightly hairs from your body. Tweezers can split that bushy beam on your face into two normal eyebrows. For you guys who don't think that they have a "uni-brow," believe me, there are likely a few hairs in that area that are worth plucking. But please, do not wax your eyebrows -- that's just taking it too far. Believe me, when someone (a girl) notices your waxed eyebrows, you will be the subject of ridicule and thought of as high maintenance -- or even as someone who possibly "bats for the other team!"

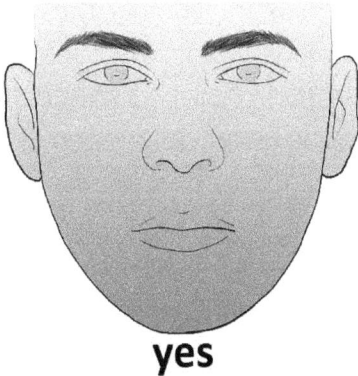 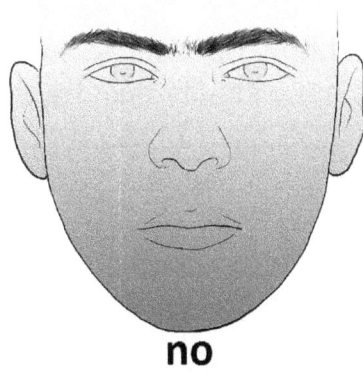

yes　　　　　　**no**

Additionally, some guys have hairy moles scattered on their bodies. Usually, each mole has a hair or two attached to it, and it's not hard to remove them. It's okay to not pluck the hair out of every single mole on your body, but it is absolutely essential that you remove any mole hairs from your face. Your face is the one part of your body that people see all the time. Needless to say, it's the first feature that girls notice on you, so it's worth investing some extra time on your face. Shaving over your moles with a razor blade isn't ideal, because the hair grows back quicker. You can do it, but do it with caution. Even a tiny cut on a mole will take a significant amount of time to stop bleeding. This is the last thing you want right before you're supposed to be picking up your date. It's happened to me before. There's nothing more stressful and annoying than driving to pick a girl up, and at the same time firmly pressing a piece of toilet paper up against the bleeding area. If you do find yourself in this situation, apply the tissue firmly on your face for at least five to ten minutes. Do not take it off before this time has elapsed to check if you're still bleeding -- you will be! Had you used tweezers in this area instead of a razor blade, you'd have gone deeper towards the root of the hair. Pulling out hair by the root causes it to grow back much more slowly than by shaving it. When you shave hair with a razor blade, it grows back faster, and often thicker. They say that's an old wives tale, but why chance it?

It's also worth noting that guys should be very aware of long, unsightly nose hairs protruding from their nostrils. For a quick fix, you can purchase a pair of hair clippers that come with a nose hair trimmer, or you can purchase a tool specifically intended to deal with nose hairs. Guys must be aware of what's going on in their nostrils. Believe me: no girl is going to be turned on by that one long, ugly hair that's just begging to be removed.

Also, every guy should own at least one, if not two pairs of nail clippers. Ideally, it's good to have a regular pair for your fingernails and a larger pair for your toenails. At the bare minimum, cut your nails once a week. I like to do this every Friday, typically when I'm getting ready to go out that night. Do this either before you shower or afterward, it doesn't matter, as long as it gets done. It's best to cut nails so that there's a thin white nail visible. You do not want to cut your nails too short. If you ever cut a nail to the point where it bleeds, you know you've gone too far. Of course, you don't want to leave the nail too long, either, so use your best judgment. This all may sound minor, but you'll want to avoid a hangnail when putting on a shirt. Even worse, you do not want to cut a girl with your big toenail while you're in bed together. It's also not a bad idea to get a manicure or pedicure. Believe it or not, guys, these aren't just for women anymore. Even if you only do it once in awhile, or even one time, you may be surprised by how much you can learn. Just by going to a professional once, you'll likely pick up a tip or two about grooming for future reference, which you can then apply to your own regular grooming habits.

For guys out there who have a wool vest on all the time, electric hair clippers are a useful tool to control the length of your chest hair. Listen, I don't decide the trends in our culture, but we're definitely not in the midst of a

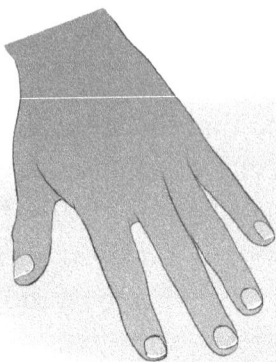 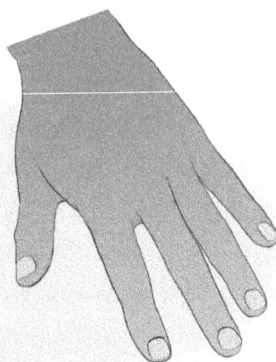

yes　　　　　　　　**no**

time period when it's manly and sexy to women for you to sport lots of chest hair. I'm not stating that all women dislike chest hair. In fact, I've met some women who absolutely love running their fingers through a man's chest hair. I also have some guy friends who love having thick chest hair. It comes down to a matter of personal preference and taste. However, I suggest that until you find yourself in a relationship with a girl who verbalizes that she loves chest hair, you should stick with a clean look. In today's society (for the most part), girls like a guy with a clean look. Plus, this look will show off your muscles more, if you happen to have any. Even if you don't have muscles, chest hair maintenance improves your appearance, thus increasing your overall confidence that much more.

After applying some of these basic grooming techniques, your t-shirt can come off more comfortably at the beach. Many guys haven't tried or even considered grooming their chest hair, but it is quite simple. First of all, please do not shave your entire chest with a razor. A great reason to avoid this is because hair growing back as stubble can be a discomfort for girls on their skin. Plus, shaving will not only make the hair grow back faster, but also thicker, coarser, and possibly even sharper. Shaving your body hair tends to lead to pimples popping up, too, with a much greater risk for ingrown hairs.

At the pool or at the beach, taking off a shirt can become very uncomfortable for guys dealing with distracting eyesores on their chests. For the majority of guys, a simple pair of electric clippers with adjustable blades will work just fine to trim chest hair. If you don't already own this item, you should pick one up; some cost as little as $20. Keep the length short by using one of the lower numbered blade settings (or no blade, for an even closer trim). Trimming your chest hair should be done about every other week or so. For guys with little chest hair or random patches, you can go ahead and remove all the hair by shaving. You might even consider an occasional waxing, if you're up for that, or laser hair removal.

Cleaning up hair at home should never be an issue. Just use some toilet paper or paper towels to wrap up the mess. However, do not flush hair down the toilet, and try not to let too much hair go down the shower or sink drain. If you don't have a broom, you should at least own a brush and dustpan to clean up the mess.

Unless you're going for something very basic and have experience with it, I strongly urge you to not use electric clippers to cut the hair on your head. The better and more logical choice is to get your hair cut by a professional. You don't have to spend $100 at a salon, because any barber will cut your hair more evenly than you could ever do. Once a month, you should make an appointment to get your hair cut at a place that you like and by someone you trust. Don't be afraid to ask the person cutting your hair what's "in" or what cut would look best on you.

It also should be pointed out that guys grow hair on the back of their necks as well. Back in college, my fraternity brother Mike often helped me out by trimming the back of my neck, and vice versa. We referred to this as "taping." Taping is always a good idea, because it's nice to get rid of unwanted neck hair with electric clippers or a razor, between haircuts. If you don't already trim that area yourself, consider asking your roommate, friend, or girlfriend to help you out.

Let's go down south now. Do you like girls who shave everything, have runways, or who are neatly trimmed? If so, you shouldn't be afraid of doing some trimming on yourself. This is something that I thought I would never do. I never ever imagined that I'd have any type of sharp object below the beltline. However, one day I finally took a chance and shaved my entire pubic area. Trust me, the rumor that it does look bigger upon completion is true, and after a shower, the region also dries immediately. In addition, the feeling is incredible when your clean pubic area rubs against her oh-so-smooth and soft areas. It's also a courtesy to your girl because you're not making her deal with a forest down there. At first, you may suffer a few battle scars, but I promise that in time you will find a method that works best for you. I recommend doing this about once a week.

You might want to "rub one out" before you begin this special shaving experience. Flaccid and loose will make for an easier experience as well, especially when you shave those few little hairs at the base of your shaft by your stomach. Skin is easier to shave when it's stretched, making it easier to do an even job, and it's a good idea to use shaving gel or cream, but be careful to not use too much cream because you want to be able to see what you're shaving. If you lather up too much, you might end up shaving parts of your stomach and legs. We're going for symmetry here. After you shower and dry yourself off completely, apply baby powder to the area. This is a must. Use a little bit to cover the sensitive spots and to prevent little bumps and breakouts; it also will help deal with any slight bleeding. Baby powder is also healthy for the skin in general. It will prevent irritation from your underwear or pants, should you prefer going commando.

Just to be clear, I'm not demanding that all guys shave their entire pubic regions. For me, I like both the look and feel. I've received positive feedback from women whom I've dated, too. Most of them expressed appreciation that I took the time to groom. But again, if you don't want to shave everything, that's fine. If you want to just trim, that's okay too; it's all up to you.

For guys who have a hairy ass and have thought about shaving it, I warn you -- do not shave it with a razor blade. The hair will grow back quicker, thicker, and sharper. When ass hair grows back, it causes major discomfort when sitting in the car, a classroom, on a couch, or anywhere for that matter. Trust me, I found out the hard way. You will have irritation, and your ass will look like it is coming down with chicken pox. You'll be itching like crazy, too, as if you actually had the chicken pox. Nothing is worse than scratching constantly or squirming back and forth in your chair, and having the girl next to you wondering what you're doing. Good luck trying to explain that one to her!

If you want to take your electric clippers to your behind, I suggest keeping the blade number at a one or a two to avoid the after-effects of a razor blade. There's still risk with using clippers, so proceed with care! If you really want to thoroughly remove all of your ass hair, I suggest regular waxing. Most professional waxing specialists charge between $20 and $50 for this treatment, depending on the amount of surface area covered.

I do not recommend using over-the-counter self-waxing materials or substances for self-waxing anywhere on your body. Some time ago, I purchased a self-waxing machine and tried it on my upper pubic area. Not only does the wax burn your skin, it's a huge hassle to get the wax from the machine to the intended area on your body. During the process, I found it very challenging to not make a huge mess. It was difficult to get the wax where it needed to go, and much of it ended up in the sink, on the floor, or in contact with unintended body parts. The clean-up took longer than the waxing process, including the time it took to go to the store to purchase the materials. Be careful with Nair, too, because people have mixed results using it. Please remember that everyone's skin does not react in the same way. Before using any of these products, talk to your doctor or dermatologist. Be smart: if usage leads to pain, discomfort, or any noticeable skin problems, immediately stop using the product and seek medical attention.

* * *

Like your car and home, you must take care of yourself. It's beneficial to your body and mind to be routinely active. I recommend that everybody make time for an exercise routine that works best for them. In an effort to keep this section simple, all you really need to focus on are these three goals -- burning calories, building muscle, and having a reasonable diet.

There are countless ways that you can burn calories. Jogging, running, and even walking are okay, but if you enjoy playing sports, soccer or basketball burns lots of calories too. Whether on a treadmill, in a swimming pool, or on a bicycle, figure out what you enjoy the most then make a serious commitment to staying determined and focused.

In terms of building muscle, regardless of what you do to accomplish this, once again, commitment will be the most important factor in determining how fit you become. It doesn't hurt to do pushups, crunches, and lunges before you jump into the shower or go to bed. It doesn't matter what time of day you do this, but being on a routine is essential. Three sets of 12 for each of these basic exercises will help you build and maintain muscle tone.

If you stumble upon a gym membership card, it doesn't hurt to use it! If traveling to a gym is not in your interest or budget, you don't need an oversized workout center at home to become more muscular. If used properly and habitually, a few dumbbells can go a long way. Any sporting goods store has plenty of useful fitness items for sale. In addition to weights, exercise balls, benches and pull up bars are also convenient tools for at-home exercise.

One product that I highly recommend is the Iron Gym™ pull up bar. It fits tightly in your doorframe and requires minimal assembly -- no screws or nails needed!

With multiple grips, it's a wonderful way to build your upper body. In addition, you can tone your lower abs by using the Velcro ab straps. Lower abs tends to be a problematic area for most guys to develop. Guys accumulate more fat on their bellies than anywhere else on their bodies. Remember, though, without consistent calorie-burning exercises (cardio), all the ab work in the world won't help you. Sure, you'll build up stomach muscles, but they will remain hidden underneath a layer of fat.

Don't forget that before doing any sort of weight lifting or cardiovascular activity, you must first do a few minutes of basic stretching. This will help minimize the risk of a pulled muscle or other injury. If you're new to working out, be sure to take it slow and not overdo it. Repetitions should be fluid; remember to exhale when weight goes up, and inhale as the weight is slowly let down. Correct breathing is of utmost importance.

Girls tend to be more attracted to guys who are toned and fit. Forgetting others for a moment, it's important that you are healthy and feel good about yourself, for yourself. For ages, people have tried to figure out what the ideal diet is. I'd like to pass along a few quick tips about healthy eating habits. First of all, despite a huge temptation in our society, you must avoid fast food at all costs. (In-N-Out Burger is the only exception!) Seriously though, if you indulge in this type of grub, please do so infrequently. This goes for any food that is high in fat, sugar, and/or sodium. From my personal experience with a nutritionist, I've learned that staying away from foods that have artificial flavorings and preservatives, while including organic foods in your diet, will lead to a healthier lifestyle. If you can't cut junk food out entirely, be reasonable with your overall consumption of it.

It's not my place to tell you that you must eat all organic this or consume "x" amount of calories daily. I do recommend, though, that guys eat foods containing high amounts of protein. Chicken, fish, turkey, and lean steaks are all high in protein with limited amounts of fat. The key to healthy eating habits is to have a balanced diet, so be sure to eat plenty of fruits and vegetables throughout the day. Drink lots of water too! Try to be disciplined by avoiding late night snacking. The closer to bed time that you eat, the harder it is for your inactive body to burn calories. Eating before bed will also make it harder to fall asleep, with your internal system so active. Getting a good night's sleep is essential to maintaining good health.

In an effort to protect you, and also myself, I want to reiterate that I'm not a professional in the areas of fitness or nutrition. My intentions are merely to give you a foundation on which to build and find a system of diet and exercise that suits your needs. Everybody is built differently, and I urge you to talk to physicians, trainers, nutritionists, or any other applicable experts.

The most important thing is to follow through with your commitment to your goals by sticking to a routine. With all this talk about health and fitness, I don't want you to feel overwhelmed. While I deeply value the importance of taking care of my body, do not interpret my writings as a declaration that you must have the body of a Calvin Klein underwear model. Please do not starve yourself in an attempt to get a washboard stomach. Real change takes time and requires patience. I promise you that if you make the choice to apply yourself and to live a generally healthy lifestyle, you will achieve significant results.

Now, let us talk about how to dress. I'm not referring to what you might wear to work or to the gym -- I'm talking about what to wear on a Friday or Saturday night when you have plans to go out (on a date even). You might not have the mindset of going out to meet somebody, but you never know when you will, so it's always best to be prepared and to dress appropriately.

Own at least two pairs of designer brand jeans -- not the kind that you find at Target. Target's a great place and has many useful items that I've previously discussed, but your "Friday night jeans" should not be Wranglers. Here are some specific examples of what I mean by designer jeans -- True Religion, Rock n' Republic, Abercrombie & Fitch, Lucky, or Diesel. There are plenty of other quality designer jeans out there, but those brands seem to be the most well known. Trust me, jeans are not just jeans. Girls will know if you're wearing a decent denim product. Some high-end pants will cost you, but they will have a long lifespan and you will get your money's worth with them.

I suggest that one pair be distressed (kneeholes or visible wear and tear), and the other clean and pristine looking. The distressed look is more appropriate for bars and other casual settings. Your traditional pair of jeans is better for clubs, lounges, and dates. Try to be aware of when sales are on, and locate some outlet stores, where manufacturers sell directly to the public through their own branded stores. In other words, there are discounts to be had.

Jeans should be long enough to nearly cover your shoes while standing or sitting, but obviously not too long to where you're mopping the floor with them. Jeans should fit low and tight on the crotch and expand slightly as the pant leg runs down to the ankle. The pants should fit firmly to your behind. Your underwear should not stick out more than an inch above the waistline of your pants. If you're buying and wearing clothing that fits you properly, the waistline of your underwear should match that of your pants or shorts. When sitting down, your pants should be long enough so that your socks aren't visible. When going out (and expecting to meet women), do not wear white socks. Black, brown, blue, or even grey socks do the trick. Unless you're moonwalking in a Pepsi commercial, please avoid white socks with dark dress shoes.

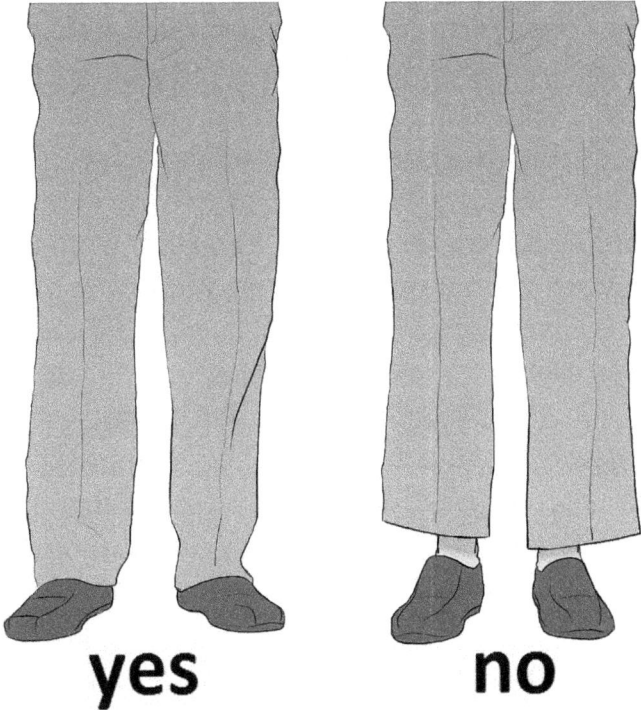

yes   no

yes   **no**

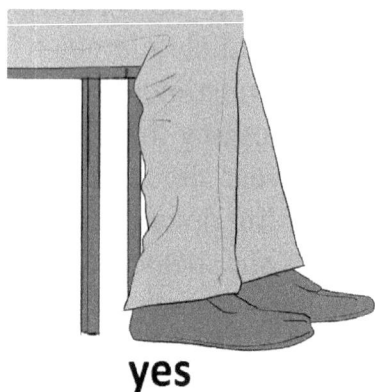

Own at least one pair of nice black dress shoes and one pair of nice brown dress shoes. Steve Madden and Doc Martin are two popular shoe brands that make quality products. You will get your money's worth with these shoes. I realize that I talk a lot about specific brands, and I do acknowledge that there are plenty of other options for you in terms of name brand clothing and footwear. Any brands mentioned in this book should be used as a starting point and not as a be-all, end-all for what you purchase.

If you clean your shoes regularly using shoe polish, they'll last much longer. Look at your shoes before you go out and ask, "Would a shoeshine make them look better?" Shine your shoes on an as needed basis. Check the bottoms of your footwear for gum or anything else that could get stuck to them. If anything gross is on your shoes, remove it. Grab a butter knife, paper towels, or whatever it takes to get the job done. Goo-gone or any other citrus-based solution does a good job when it comes to removing sticky stuff. The bottom line is this: guys, take care of your stuff!

Another accessory that you should own is a belt, and it should be leather. A rule of thumb is to always match the color of your belt to the color of your shoes. Brown shoes = brown belt, black shoes = black belt.

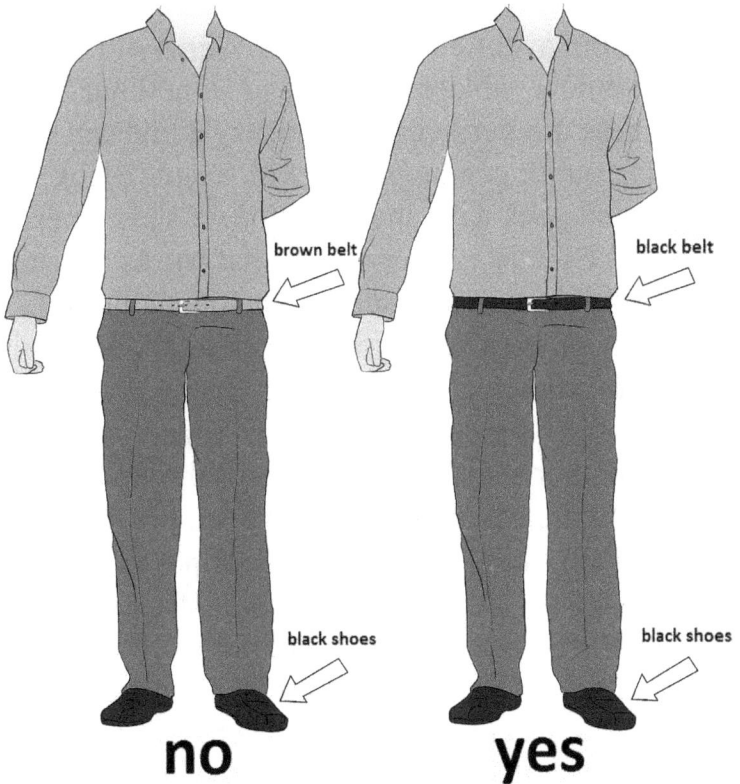

brown belt

black belt

black shoes

black shoes

no   **yes**

I had better not catch you owning a reversible belt that is black on one side and brown on the other. You might not think that people know it's a reversible belt, but trust me, they do. It's really tacky, and you're better off leaving it in your father's closet next to his other old fashioned belts. If you're reading this book and realize that you're either wearing one of these belts or have one of them in your closet, quickly bookmark this page, go to the store and get a new belt now. I will wait…

Now, assuming that you've obtained another belt, immediately throw the old belt away, because it isn't even worth donating.

Every guy should own between four and eight buttoned down cotton dress shirts. Three of these should be solid colors -- black, white, and something like a sky blue. These are very versatile shirts. White can be used for going out or can be paired with a suit. Black is always in style and goes with any occasion. It's even perfect for a funeral! Blue is a cheery color that works especially well for daytime events such as banquets, family occasions, or even some job interviews. A blue shirt is also appropriate for Thanksgiving dinner, or when you're meeting a girl's parents for the first time.

Another example of a cotton shirt that you should own is a white collared shirt with a simple design or pattern, such as light blue vertical stripes or boxes. A black shirt with either white or silver stripes is also a good look. As important as it is to wear clothes that are stylish, it won't matter if you buy the most expensive shirt if it doesn't fit you well. Guys have a tendency to either wear clothes that are too baggy, or in an attempt to show off their physique, clothes that are too tight. A shirt should be form fitting, but it shouldn't cut off your circulation. Wear clothes that fit you! If you're not sure if something fits correctly, get a second opinion before you buy it.

I advise you to dry clean your cotton shirts and any

other garments that require dry cleaning. Machine washing often causes colors to fade. It also doesn't hurt to own and use a lint brush. If you realize that you've used your last strip on the lint brush, an alternative is to use tape to remove hair or lint from clothing. Even though various kinds of tape might work, I recommend regular Scotch tape. I forewarn you that it's a slow process and will require a lot of tape.

Most of the time, you do not need to tuck in a dress shirt. If it's a normal bar night, dinner with friends, or even a date, you can keep your shirt untucked. Tucking in your shirt can send out misleading signals. People (girls) might interpret a guy with a tucked-in shirt as someone who is uptight, overly professional, or even high maintenance. It's just not a good look outside of a corporate work environment. Obviously, if you are going to an event or a place that requires formal wear, then please tuck in your shirt. Don't be the idiot who's trying to be unique by going against the dress code and having your shirt hanging out. If the place requires a tie, then you must tuck in your shirt.

yes

no

no

yes

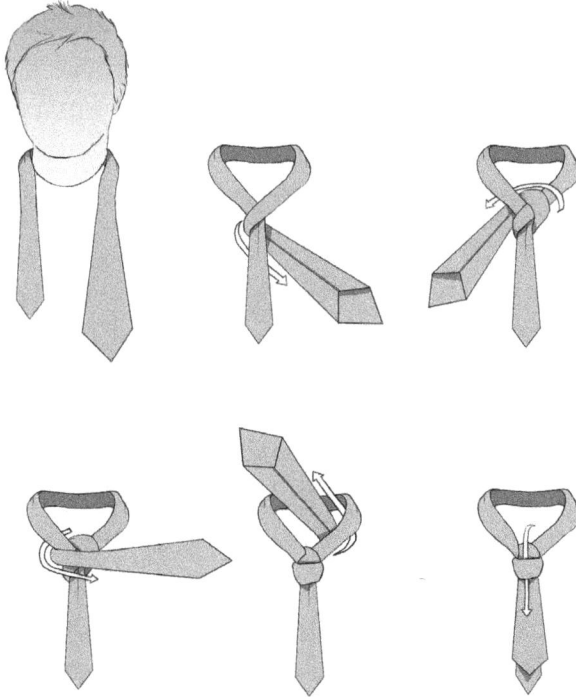

Guys, you don't need to wear a hundred rings all over your fingers. It's okay to wear a ring or even two, but don't overdo it. A nice silver watch such as a Fossil, Oakley, or Nike brand is an accessory that adds to your overall appearance. This may sound obvious, but your watch should actually work, too, just in case somebody asks you for the time. Who knows, a girl asking you for the time could serve as a nice conversation starter. As far as earrings go, they aren't for me, but if they work for you, go for it. Be who you are.

The key is to stick with what works for you. Use my words as a guide, but don't forget to be yourself too! Listen, guys, I know fashion is very trendy and is constantly evolving and changing, and I don't expect you to keep up. However, do not wear clothing that is ten-plus years old and looks it. I can't stress enough the importance of making sure your clothes fit properly. If you don't already know this, please be aware that your work clothes, going out clothes, sleeping, and working out clothes should definitely not all be one and the same.

* * *

Now that you've showered, have on your designer jeans, collared shirt, freshly shined shoes (with non-white socks and matching belt), it's time to apply a small amount of cologne. One spray in the front and one spray in back is enough to last an evening. The amount you put on should probably be enough for her to smell you from three feet away. Wearing too much means that people can pick up the scent from five feet away or more. Always remember that people should only smell your cologne when they get close to you. That's no more than two sprays. Popular (yet affordable) colognes are Tommy Hilfiger, Calvin Klein, or even Abercrombie. When buying cologne, don't be afraid to sample a few to find out what you like the most. Please do not use an old musky bottle that you found in your grandfather's cabinet -- unless you want to smell like him too!

Before you head out the door, don't forget to carry gum with you. I suggest that you avoid breath sprays, unless you're Jim Carrey in "Dumb & Dumber." Breath sprays don't last as long as gum and mints do. At all times, keep an extra pack of gum or mints in your car in case of an emergency. Usually, needing gum isn't considered an emergency, but when you're picking a girl up and you're almost at her place, you don't want to suddenly remember that your pack of Wrigley's is sitting on the counter top back at home. If this happens, it will then feel like an emergency.

There's one more thing we should discuss before you head out the door -- condoms. The purpose of this book isn't to help you have a one-night stand on a Friday night. However, anytime you go out in hopes of having sex, or with the knowledge that there is a realistic chance that you could have sex, definitely carry a condom(s) with you.

Later in the book, I'll discuss going on dates and certain philosophies I have about carrying condoms on dates. But, if you're going out with a "good girl" on a first date, you probably aren't going to have sex that night.

Just as a reminder: anytime you carry condoms, there's a small chance that one could accidentally fly out of your pocket when you're reaching for your wallet. Always know when you have protection on you. You don't want to be reaching for your wallet to pay the bill at dinner and have a condom fly out by mistake. If this happens and your date catches a glimpse of your Trojans, she might be insulted by your revealed expectations for the evening. Most girls don't want to be perceived as "easy," so be aware when you have condoms on you. Even if you grab a flying condom before a girl notices, quickly hiding it could make you look shady.

Even though "flying condoms" is an unlikely scenario, there's a chance it won't bother a girl at all if she finds out you have condoms on you. In fact, she might even appreciate your preparedness and show of responsibility. The bottom line is to always be prepared when there's any chance of having sex. You can always hope that a girl has some kind of contraception at her place, but it's best not to assume and it's better to be safe than sorry!

Chapter 3: The Wingman and Wing-girl

Hopefully by now, I've given you a pretty good foundation in terms of what you need for your home and the essentials you should have. Now, it's time to get out there and put yourself in the line of fire. Let's try to meet girls who you once thought were out of your league. At some point, likely sooner than later, you'll want to bring these girls back to your tidy and inviting home. After all, I'm sure that most of you guys who bought this book are eager to find out the best ways to approach girls.

So, it's Friday night, your long work week is over, and you're ready to go out and have a good time and hopefully meet some single women. The next step is to make sure that you go out with a wingman. A wingman is someone who you consider to be a friend -- a person with whom you have a good rapport. Somebody you've just met or barely hung out with does not make for a good wingman, because he might say or do something that could be embarrassing or offensive. A bad wingman can quickly ruin any potential chemistry with a female you might be interested in, or one who might be interested in you. If your friend is a douchebag, and this girl is just meeting you, what could that make you by association?

Speaking from personal experience, an example of a poor excuse for a wingman was a neighbor I ran into at a local establishment, a few days after meeting him in the apartment complex laundry room. I was at a bar with a couple of friends when I approached an attractive girl who was standing nearby. I introduced myself, and the conversation seemed to be going very well, when about five minutes in, out of the blue, I heard my name yelled loudly, "Lance!" Being in the midst of dialogue with a prospect, I ignored the first call. "Lance!" It came louder and clearer the second time. He approached me, and in a lame pimp-daddy tone, was all like, "What's up man? How's it goin'? Who's this lady friend of yours?" This might sound relatively harmless, but just picture some wannabe player hurting your chances of getting with a girl you find attractive. Not to mention, this person acted like we'd been best friends for years.

Then he said to me (with the girl standing right there), "Damn, she's hot. Good job." I then thought to myself, "Wow, this guy is clueless." I can only imagine what the girl was thinking about me right then, just by association. When you first meet someone, there are certain words and phrases that should be avoided, such as, "You're a hot girl." It's more complimentary to say something like "You're pretty" or "Wow, you're a beautiful girl." Some may find the lines I suggest to be cheesy, but I'd rather be cheesy and honest than say something callous like, "Wow, you're totally hot." Not that it's inherently wrong to use the word "hot," or to call a girl "hot," but there's just a time and a place for it, and the first few minutes of meeting somebody is usually not that time.

It's always a good idea to have a wingman that knows how to read a situation and act accordingly. For the ideal wingman, you'll want to team up with a friend who knows you but is also interested in the opposite type of girl. For example, I tend to be attracted to blonde-haired, blue-eyed petite girls (but not all the time and not exclusively). I know it's a cliché to say that I have a certain "type," especially since I've often dated outside of it, but there's nothing wrong with being predominantly more attracted to a specific kind of girl when it comes to physical appearance. Often, my chops have been busted over this, but everybody has their preferences and quirks when it comes to attraction to the opposite sex. If you and your wingman have different tastes, you guys will be able to help each other out that much more. In any event, what's most important is to always be on the same page with your wingman. Communicate. Let your wingman know which girl at the bar catches your eye. You want to avoid awkward tension with any person who's a good friend.

To give an example, I was at a bar with a favorite wingman of mine, David. I made eye contact with two girls across the room. One girl was blonde and the other was a brunette. They were both very attractive, well, at least from a distance. But hey, many girls look good from a distance! David and I decided to approach these girls. The closer we got, the more attractive they became, and no, we weren't at the point of having beer goggles on just yet!

Immediately, David walked up to the brunette, leaving the blonde open for me. This was a textbook maneuver by a seasoned wingman, making it easy for me to initiate conversation with the girl whom I was interested in from the get-go. Because my wingman was already talking to her friend, she was comfortable talking to me, because she didn't have to worry about her friend. There wasn't a third-wheel or awkward situation because two conversations were occurring simultaneously, and my wingman and I never took these girls out of their comfort zone. Gentleman, this is something I will talk about in greater detail very shortly, so take note because this is key: if you are able to keep a girl feeling like she's in control and in her comfort zone, by feeling respected, this will better your odds of leaving the bar with her phone number.

The scenarios that I described above are ideal situations. However, more often than not, when two guys meet two girls at the same time, the result will be that all four people will have one conversation together at first, and that's just as good to start the night off.

Don't forget that you're a wingman too! Not every night is going to be about you and your needs; you should definitely reciprocate. If the girl your friend likes is conversing with you, speak highly of him. Without being rude or too obvious, you can ask the girl questions about her friend -- the one you like. Don't make it the first topic of conversation, but ask questions that make it apparent that you're clearly interested in the friend. This will help leave the door open for your wingman.

Also, if the girl that you're talking to isn't your type or is off-putting in some way, but you see your wingman making strides with his girl, go ahead and take one for the team. This doesn't mean that you have to sleep with the girl, but do keep up the conversation, with your wingman's best interest in mind. Plus, it's good practice talking to girls. You have nothing to lose, and you should chalk it up as invaluable experience.

A good wingman pays close attention to not only the conversation he's having with the girl he likes, but when possible, he also follows what you and the girl you like are saying. In general, it's important that all four people become friendly with one another -- and that should be a standard that good wingmen live by.

Now, let's talk about a different type of wingman: a female wingman, or what I like to call a "wing-girl." A wing-girl is a close female friend who is usually on the same page personality-wise. It doesn't hurt to have a wing-girl who is physically attractive. Let's face it: when a guy enters a room with an attractive girl, whether the guy is with the girl or not, it forces other people in the room to notice the guy and become intrigued by him.

This is a girl whose friendship you value more than potential sex with her. You might love to sleep with your wing-girls, but let me be honest here -- risking a hard-to-find, potentially lifelong friendship just isn't worth it. That's my opinion. If you spend a significant amount of time with your wing-girl, and over a period of years develop a close friendship, certain strong feelings will grow. If the chemistry is there and it feels right, I hope for nothing short of a fairy tale ending for you and your soon-to-be (ex)wing-girl.

Guys, this may sound ridiculous to you, but hey, that's life, and a part of growing up and becoming a young adult. You're not in college, and you Greek people know exactly what I'm referring to when I mention hooking up with your sorority little sister. You know that you're breaking an unwritten code when you cross that line. It's kind of the same way with wing-girls. Also, respecting your wing-girls will help set up a nice foundation for a future life in which you will have many friends of the opposite sex. Keeping your hands off a wing-girl helps you control your sexual desires for forbidden women that you are going to spend lots of time around: coworkers, your significant others' friends, even girls at the gym, or any other female who could potentially ruin the part of your life that is sacred to you when you're in a committed relationship. Know what's appropriate and where the line is by keeping yourself in check.

I want to talk about a good experience that I had with a wing-girl, so that you can gain a better understanding of the value of a wing-girl. So often, she went out on a limb for me by doing things that I would have never been able to do for myself -- well, at least not sober. A wing-girl who I am still friends with to this day is a perfect example of someone I care deeply about. She's not only physically beautiful, but also beautiful on the inside. She possesses all the traits that I admire, and she is definitely someone I trust. Her word is worth more than gold. I admit that not every wing-girl is going to be exactly like her, but girls like her are out there for you to find.

Let me share a story about my wing-girl, Crystal, who has helped me out in countless situations when I was trying to meet girls. Just the other night, I was out at the bar with her when I saw my typical blonde-haired, blue-eyed dream girl walk past me and head towards the restroom. I considered waiting by the restroom for her to come out, but that would have been too creepy. As I was pondering my choices, Crystal asked me, "Why didn't you try to talk to her?" Before I could even respond, she was headed off to the restroom to do research on my behalf.

After a few minutes, I saw her walking out with the girl! They even looked like they were having a fun conversation. Next thing you know, they approached me. Crystal then introduced me to "Jill," and explained that she was here with a group of her friends and that she had just gotten out of a relationship. That meant that she was single, and tonight she most likely just wanted to have a good time with her friends. She was probably looking for somebody to mingle and relax with.

The key points to this story are: a beautiful girl walked by me and I was unable to articulate the right words within a small window of opportunity. Crystal, being the kick-ass wing-girl that she is, sensed her window of opportunity to help was closing quickly as well. Without hesitation and on my behalf, she, like all good wing-girls, found out information about this girl for me. She got the whole scoop -- her name, her purpose for being out, who she was with, and if she was taken. Crystal accomplished this mission quickly, whereas for most guys it would take several drinks or a couple of hours to even come close to Crystal's record-breaking time. This is just one of the many times when a wing-girl of mine has instinctively reacted like a good-natured friend.

One thing that you never want to do is piss off your wing-girl while you're out together. Do not make her feel like she's being used or ignored at any time throughout the evening. Incorporate your wing-girl into conversations, buy her a few drinks, and find out if there's anybody she's interested in. Return the favor for her. Guys, please don't leave the bar without letting your wing-girl know that you're headed elsewhere. Make sure that she has a safe ride home by giving her money for a cab, which is always a kind gesture. Especially consider doing this if your wing-girl helped you out that night. A good wing-girl will always find out the crucial information for you and then introduce you to the girls you like. The bottom line is: your wingman and wing-girl deserve your respect and appreciation.

51

Chapter 4: Dating and the Internet

We are in the midst of a time period when social networking is wildly popular, and more than likely the majority of the people we meet will have their own Facebook page, or whatever is popular at the time when you're reading this book. Most people search for the page of someone they just met, as soon as they get home from the bar. With iPhones, Droids, Blackberrys, and all other forms of technology, it's easy to check our social media pages, even while we're on the move. Besides checking out her photos, believe it or not you can use other information listed on a girl's page to your advantage. You don't have to be a detective (or even worse -- a stalker/psychotic) when it comes to glancing at a person's Facebook page, but there are some red flags you might want to look out for. I'm here to help you more easily distinguish potentially hazardous items that can pop up on a girl's social networking page, things that could come back to haunt you.

One thing to look for is in the first section that we guys will go to on her page -- her photo albums. If she has countless photos of her and a bunch of dudes, this isn't a very good sign that she's looking for a serious relationship -- especially if these types of photos are all that she posts. If she appears inebriated in many of the pictures, or many of them are of her toasting or taking shots, take this into consideration when thinking about expectations for her.

Photo comments and general comments can sometimes be just as telling as photographs. Take note if a girl has many comments that she probably wouldn't want her mother to see. We're all adults who can appreciate a crude joke here and there, but if a young lady's page is littered with vulgar and obscene material, be aware of that. It is up to you to determine what your threshold for this type of Internet display is. What's over the top and offensive to one person might not come across exactly the same way to another.

Let's say a girl has a comment on her page left by a guy, and it reads something along the lines of, "Hey babe, I had a good time the other night. You left your jacket here along with a few other items, wink." This could be a harmless, innocent joke, but it could carry meaning, too, in the sense that it might not be so challenging for you to get in her pants. Keep in mind that this could be a singular comment, but if she has these kinds of comments all over her page, although it's not entirely impossible, you probably shouldn't expect to be in a serious relationship with her soon.

Among the more obvious signs is a bunch of slutty photographs; I shouldn't have to tell you that this should serve as a warning. If a girl proudly displays an inordinate amount of photos of her alone, she might be in love with herself. If a girl has lots of flyers or club promotion icons on her page, take this as a sign that she likes to go out a lot. At this point in her life, she's all about meeting new people. Just be advised, a girl like this probably isn't seeking a committed relationship.

Looking at her photos will remind you of her attractiveness, but they also might trigger your memory to recall information that could be helpful in the future. Instead of using her photos merely to "check her out," click around and see if she has any photos posted with her siblings, parents, or any other family. This could be a telling sign of what's important to her.

Although photographs, posts, and comments are probably more telling, some of the more trivial information shared on the Internet can be helpful too. Do not read a girl's Facebook page, memorize every band she likes, and then bring up these musical acts immediately in conversation the next time you talk to her. You want to avoid being too specific about these things, because you'll come off as a stalker, and this will definitely take her out of that all-important comfort zone. If she brings up that her favorite movie is "Titanic," obviously you can discuss that. Don't overwhelm her, and be judicious with your use of trivial items she lists on her page. To reiterate: do not forcefully bring up her favorite books, music, movies, or TV shows, but ask a couple of general questions. When you finally do go on a date with her, posing questions like, "Do you have any favorite TV shows?" is fine. You can use information that you already know about her to your advantage, without making it come across as creepy and researched.

You should also consider her search for your personal page and scrutinizing it too. Think for a moment about all the things that you share with people on the Internet. Whether or not you have a private profile or a public one, at some point she's going to see your social media page. We as guys have to assume that she will be (in many ways) judging us, and likely based on the same criteria that we use to judge her. Be smart about the things you share, and think about what's on your page that might turn girls off.

Just as we examined red flags on her page, put yourself in her shoes, now looking at your page. How does it look to a girl who might be interested in dating you when she sees lots of females leaving comments on your page that may be sexual in nature? I'm not saying that you need to make your profile completely private or G-rated, or that you must delete countless old comments, but it doesn't hurt to do a basic clean-up once in awhile if you have anything overwhelmingly self-incriminating on your page that you feel misrepresents you.

Earlier, we analyzed the power of a good wing-girl, and yes, it's true that girls tend to be intrigued by guys who are around other girls, especially attractive ones. However, there may be a time when this kind of display (whether in person or on the Internet) could come across as obnoxious. She could wonder about whether you're insecure, given your need to always have women around you. She could also conclude that you're an attention-whore. Most girls who are looking for something serious are not going to be interested in a guy who tries to come across as a pimp, player, or even worse, a man-whore. Even a comment left on your social media page that could seem completely harmless like, "luv u, miss u" can lead to a misinterpreted message. If you're the type of guy who says things like "luv u," or even "love you" very casually, these types of phrases can lose their meaning, value, and significance. In addition, be careful when using terms like, "babe," "cutie," "honey," "sweetie" and so on. Even though these terms may seem harmless to you, in a girl's eyes they might carry entirely different connotations.

Say you're in a relationship and you're telling your girlfriend that you love her, or even simply that you miss her. If she sees your comments on another girl's page with similar phrases, even if it's in a different context, you need to think about how your girlfriend is going to feel. Be aware of what you say to your female friends online, and how in turn that could make someone you're dating feel.

If you have photos on your page of female friends, or even exes, this could give any new girl the impression that you are merely a player, and that she has reason to question your character, which could lead to the assumption that you're not over past relationships.

This kind of thing happened to me. I met a girl at a local bar in Hollywood. Her name was Renee. She was 24, had cute brown bangs and big blue eyes -- very attractive. I approached her and we talked for a bit. We seemed to be hitting it off pretty well. Numbers were exchanged, followed by a warm goodbye hug. I felt that a goodbye peck on the cheek in this case would be well received. So, I went for it, and she responded positively with a smile.

Of course, shortly after I returned home, I found her profile on Facebook. It was a minor miracle that I remembered her last name -- that's right, even though throughout this book you will see that I tell you to remember what females say, it's always easier said than done! The next day, I sent her a friend request with a message that was both simple and friendly. I told her I had had a good time with her and asked how her day was going.

At this point, she had probably found my profile too, because while referencing my comments and photos, she texted back, "Hmmm, you got a lot of girls on your page I see." My last five comments were from girls, true, but in my mind they were relatively harmless. Renee, though, was clearly bothered. She jumped to conclusions and was turned off by all the comments from other girls, and she was starting to be turned off by me as well.

So, I had a decision to make -- I could accept that our relationship wasn't going to go anywhere, move on and not respond, or I could take a chance and give it one more shot. Here's how it all played out -- there was a little more texting the following week, but I wasn't getting back the positive vibes that I was hoping for. She texted a remark about the "luv u/miss u" stuff on my Facebook page. Red flags began to pop up in the form of sly jests from her via text message. I knew that she was harping on the content of my page, and based on it was being overly quick to judge me. She looked at my page and chose to not go out with me.

Here's what I learned -- there isn't a right or wrong reaction to this situation. It was more about decisions, and what a person is looking for at that moment in life. If s/he isn't looking for anything serious, s/he needn't be as aware of certain comments that are visible to the public on the given page. Just remember, it's probably unfair to judge a girl too harshly for content on her page if you're not even considering what's on yours; it goes both ways.

We've talked about how social networking can affect how guys and girls interact. Always trust your judgment, and don't be afraid to give someone the benefit of the doubt. You mustn't be afraid to give a new person the chance to get to know you better. This goes for both sexes. You can learn a fair amount from a person's Facebook page, but don't take everything you see and read entirely to heart. At the end of the day, you really don't know this person well, and you shouldn't be judging anyone so harshly after having just met him or her.

Remember that there's no reason to "friend" a girl the second after you meet her. What is your ultimate goal? If you have a romantic interest in a girl, don't worry about being her friend on Facebook. If you spend enough time together, eventually you will connect on the Internet as well. You're better off waiting to friend her after the first date, or at the very least after a couple of phone conversations. Then, add her if you feel the need to. Who knows, maybe she'll make the move and add you as a friend first.

* * *

Before we move ahead into the next chapter, I want to touch on Internet dating and using dating websites. I've never been one to date via the Internet. People are never quite what they initially seem to be in photographs and profiles. Who knows how old those pictures are? In person, people never look like they did a decade ago. I'm sure that you've even seen girls post a bunch of group photos, making it a challenge to figure out whose profile it is.

I'm aware that many people have found happiness through the Internet; millions have success with sites like Match.com, eHarmony, and even Jdate. However, dating via the Internet is just not for me, at least not at the moment. I lean more toward the old school mentality of meeting girls the old fashioned way -- in person. There's just something more real, spontaneous, romantic and even magical when meeting someone in person for the first time. Meeting a potential boyfriend or girlfriend via the Internet does have its pluses, but there's something too calculated about the whole idea to me.

I take pride in being a social person. Sometimes it might be difficult to do, but it's always best to put yourself out there by making new friends. You can meet someone special through your friends. For me, it doesn't matter if it's at restaurants, bars, house parties, supermarkets, the beach, the gym, or even at work. It's possible to meet girls anywhere -- if you keep your eyes open. Yes, I know that by including work among the places where you can meet a special someone, I contradict some of my philosophies that you'll read later in this book, but hey, sometimes love comes with challenging obstacles, and we just have to go with it.

Some people are against dating coworkers, as some people aren't keen on dating on the Internet. I say: to each their own. What's most important is that you be comfortable with your approach to dating, and putting yourself in the best position to meet new people. It doesn't matter if you meet someone through the Internet or at a party, most of what I'll discuss in the following chapters will apply to you.

Chapter 5: Making an Approach

Now that you understand the concept of a good wing-person, it's appropriate to talk about how to approach the type of girl you find attractive, especially if you have never had the necessary tools or knowledge to engage in conversation.

Remember -- please don't have unrealistic expectations about clubs or bars. Most people will not meet their future girlfriend or boyfriend in a bar. Having said that, you will find that many of the same principles that we're going to discuss, believe it or not, can also apply to situations in your daily life outside of a bar or club.

My definition of a club is: any place where the majority of the clientele are on the dance floor and the music makes hearing nearly impossible, to the point where you can't even ask a simple question to the person next to you that would require more than a couple of words to answer. Take clubs for what they are -- they're places to go to drink and have fun with your friends, and maybe even hook up with someone, if that's what you choose to do.

If you've met a girl in a club environment, you might not have a lot in common with her. The odds of anything substantial developing are minimal. You shouldn't, however, rule out the miniscule percentage that a relationship could develop. Once in a blue moon, people actually do meet in bars or clubs, and it works out. But realistically, the chances of you meeting your next serious girlfriend at a club are very slim.

* * *

So, what's the first thing you do when you walk into an establishment? The first thing that guys normally do is go straight to the bar for a drink. I like to take a walk around the bar area first to see if I can find a good opening to get a drink, while at the same time looking for a prospect to chat up. Prior to the bartender serving you, it's always a smart idea to take a moment to survey the bar area.

If you see an attractive girl grabbing a drink at the bar, you don't have to sprint over right away. Let the environment dictate how quickly you travel over to her. If the bar that you're in isn't crowded, give her some space. If the girl isn't surrounded by crowds of dudes and doesn't seem to be in a rush to leave the bar, then it's no problem for you to finish your drink with your wingman first before heading over to meet her. If you're operating in a tightly packed environment, it's more natural to approach a girl sooner because you're going to have more competition. Sometimes it's smart to wait a moment or two, or even longer, before you make your move. Don't sit idle for too long, though, because that window of opportunity could soon close.

When you meet someone new, always be confident. It doesn't matter if you're meeting a girl who you might be interested in, or any girl for that matter. Whether it's a social situation or in a professional atmosphere, you'll always want to be confident throughout every conversation. This may sound easier said than done, but don't worry, I will do my best to assist you along the way. Everything that I'm discussing comes back to us trying to discover more concrete, efficient ways to increase your self-confidence.

The following is something that you've probably heard mentioned to you: you must try to find the balance between acting confident without acting cocky. If you make a conscious effort to try to act "too cool for school," this overcompensation is something that a girl will see right through in a heartbeat. Most girls can sniff out a guy who isn't acting like himself. They can tell when a guy is putting up a disingenuous front. You don't want girls to talk negatively about you. Any type of "too cool" behavior will lead to shooting yourself in the foot.

On the flipside, you don't want to be too shy and timid. As important as it is to not come across as too cocky, it's equally as important to not come across as "too nice." What I mean is you don't want to come across as a whimpering, overly nice guy. We'll discuss soon how to properly compliment a girl, but a common mistake many "nice guys" make is they overdo it with compliments, and girls can smell you reeking of desperation from a mile away.

To some of you this might sound like a frightening concept, but it's essential that you be true to yourself. When meeting new people, be who you are! Nobody's perfect, and it's not an easy task to truly be you all the time. An important suggestion is that you should at least try to be aware of how other people view you. Individuality is great, and it makes us unique as humans. However, etiquette has always been a big part of how society functions, so don't feel self-conscious about conforming to norms in many ways. Once again, balance is key -- the balance between being an individual and imitating others in society whom you have learned from, and admire.

Feel free to infer about the situations for the girls around you: is she with that guy? Is she having a conversation with him, but appears bored? Is she glancing around the room like you, looking to meet somebody else? "Rubbernecking," is a key concept that we will explore further. If a girl isn't making consistent eye contact with a guy (or anybody else) who she's talking to, this means that you have as good a chance as anybody to move in on that territory. I call this fair game.

Another role of the wingman is to help you approach group situations. For example, if you're out and you see a group of girls sitting or standing, engrossed in conversation, pay attention to certain signs. It may appear that they are deep into banter, but there might be a couple of rubberneckers present who are looking to meet guys. Never fly solo in this case, always approach with a wingman. Think about it -- if you approach three girls on your own, this has a high potential to turn into an awkward situation. They don't know you from Adam, and it's a difficult juggling act to maintain dialogue with multiple girls. If you approach the group with a wingman, it makes for a more comfortable situation for everyone, and it will increase your odds of something positive happening with these women.

In a post-college world, it's especially crucial not to waste any of your time on girls who are taken, engaged, or married. Even if you sense that a girl who you're interested in is about to break up with the person she's currently seeing, depending on how serious that relationship is, moving in shortly after isn't necessarily a smart move. There's a high probability that you will be a rebound for her, because it's unlikely that she's seeking a new relationship so soon after her breakup. Not enough time has passed for her to be ready to dive back into something serious. Now, if you only want to hook up and nothing more, who am I to stop you from pursuing it? However, if you think that a girl in this situation is going to go from one serious relationship right into the next, the odds are not in your favor.

The following is intended especially for you younger guys in your early to mid-20's: after spending the majority of your life around young people, students, and mostly single people, it's easy to forget that you're an adult now, and that some people your age are getting married. The easiest thing that you can do is to look at a girl's hand. Many guys reading this right now do not know on which hand and which finger engagement rings and wedding bands go.

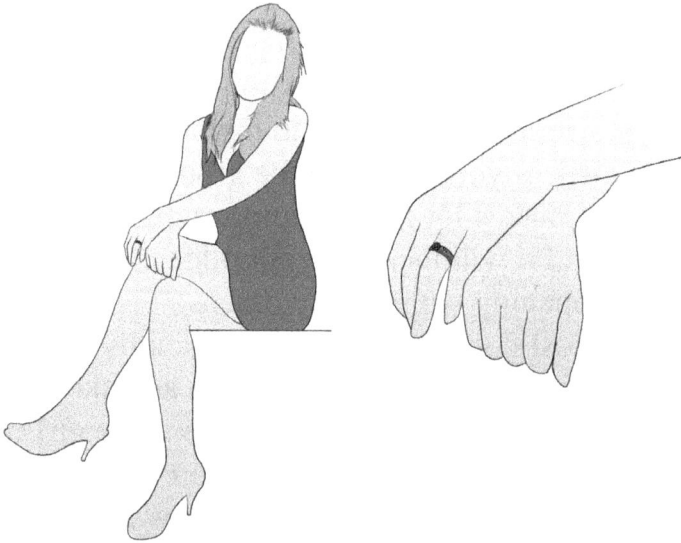

Engagement rings are typically (at the very least) a single shiny diamond that goes on the ring finger on the left hand. The wedding band, which is typically gold, white gold, or sterling silver, is a small ring often with a little protruding diamond. Wedding bands can also be found on the ring finger on the left hand. Young and recently married women will sometimes wear both their engagement ring and wedding band on the same finger. If for whatever reason you can't see a girl's hand, hopefully when you do approach her, she will say, "I'm sorry. I'm married." She might even pull her hand up to reveal the ring on her finger. Either way, you should appreciate her honesty and the fact that she isn't going to lead you on. So, while you're checking out a girl's ass or her cleavage, it's not a terrible idea to take a glance at her hand too. This saves you time, energy, and is an easy way to avoid potential disappointments. Most importantly, this habit will help keep your bar tab reasonable!

When trying to grab a drink, you don't want to go to a spot at the bar where there's a group of dudes. Look for the spot where there are a couple of girls hanging out. Order your drink. Feel out the scene. Wait for an opportunity to arise. There will be a break in their conversation. This could come when a girl orders a drink, sets her glass down, or when she's casually glancing around the room. If she's in front or behind you in a line, you can also use this as an opportunity to strike up a conversation. What I sometimes like to do is "accidentally" bump into a girl when I'm waiting at the bar to order a drink. As long as you don't actually make her spill her drink, a little innocent physical contact can be an effective way to meet a girl. Apologize for bumping into her and immediately introduce yourself.

The examples above all provide windows of

opportunity for you to initiate conversation. In the groundbreaking cinematic masterpiece "Big Daddy," it's the last tip that Adam Sandler's character shares with his young adopted son before the kid goes to sleep. "What did you learn today?" Sandler asks. Even an eight-year-old knows to reply, "Initiating the conversation is half the battle." It's something that we *all* should learn at a young age. The earlier the better, right?

If you see a group of girls talking to other guys and it seems obvious that these girls are not interested in the guys, consider buying the girls shots, or fill them up with what they're currently drinking. I realize this could lead to some awkwardness or even tension with the guys, but there's a good chance that you'll be doing these girls a favor, and sometimes it is good to go for the bold move. Don't feel bad about cock-blocking the guys. If the girls really want to continue talking to the guys, they will do just that, even after you buy them drinks.

If you can't tell what it is the girls are drinking, ask the waitress or bartender. I'm not suggesting that you always need to buy a large group of girls drinks, but if it's only two or three girls, and especially if your wingman is tied up, consider making a generous gesture. Having said that, there's absolutely nothing wrong with buying a drink for just the girl who you're most interested in meeting. This could even work to your advantage, because then there's no secret as to which one you have your eye on. After you buy this one girl a drink and have some good conversation with her and her friends, you always have the option to buy the next round for everyone.

If you see a girl who strikes your eye but she's talking to another guy, read the signs. If she's constantly fidgeting (with her phone or something else), it means that she's not in the least bit interested in the guy. If you see a girl who is constantly gripping her drink and sipping it, it means enthusiasm for the conversation isn't mutual. The quicker she's drinking, the faster she wants to get out of there. Finishing her drink acts as a good transitional moment for her to either find her friends or go to the bathroom; it gives her the opportunity for a reasonably smooth getaway. If you observe a girl exhibiting this type of behavior, don't be afraid to make your move. A moment like this provides a window of opportunity.

If you are the guy stuck with the fidgeting girl who won't put down her drink and is constantly rubber-necking, change up the conversation or get out of there as soon as possible. Find a nice break in the conversation (which shouldn't be too hard if she's rubbernecking), and say, "Oh, well listen, I'm gonna go ahead to the restroom, and we'll catch up later. It was nice to meet you." This may seem like an abrupt way to end a conversation, but remember she's the one who's being rude in the first place by rubbernecking and not giving you her undivided attention. The line I suggested above may not be your preference, but my point is that you shouldn't worry or feel guilty about leaving a situation that is a waste of your time. In fact, the girl might even become more intrigued by your ballsy move, and she might want to reconnect later that night.

In terms of changing up the conversation, you can try asking her more questions. It's also appropriate to ask, "Am I bothering you? I can leave if you'd prefer. No hard feelings." This may sound like you're swallowing your pride, but really you're showing confidence and that you're a secure person. If she's not into you, it's no skin off your back and you can continue with the rest of your evening. Always remember that even if a girl tells you that you're not bothering her, there are signals that could indicate the contrary. These signals could come in the forms of excuses, such as her telling you, "Oh, I'm waiting for my friends," or "Sorry, I have to go make a phone call now." Nine times out of ten, a girl will not be interested in you if she's using these excuses or similar ones to get away from you.

If you get caught staring at a girl near you (which means you've locked eyes), do not be the first person to turn away. Wait for her to do it first. I understand that this is a difficult battle, which we guys normally lose, but try this approach. After your eyes and hers are focused on one another for a couple of seconds, smile at her. This lets her know that you are interested in her and that you find her physically attractive. If she smiles back, go over to her, but not right away. Take a sip of your drink and inform your wingman of your plans. Let him (or her) know which girl you're interested in without pointing. Use landmarks or her clothing to describe her, e.g., "the girl in the blue top with the silver purse" or "the blonde girl standing next to the ATM." Also, if your wingman is willing to "take one for the team," let him get a look at what soon might be in store for him.

Once you decide that it's time to walk over and talk to her, do not sit down next to her at the bar (or table), assuming that she wants you to hang out with her. Instead, simply say, "I saw you from across the room and I wanted to come over to say hi and introduce myself." When introducing myself to a girl, what I like to do is extend my right arm for a handshake (keep eye contact while doing this), and then after she puts her hand in mine, I follow up by covering her hand with my left hand. Guys, there should be a definite difference when it comes to shaking hands with girls versus shaking hands with other guys. With other guys, you want to be strong and firm, but you want to be gentler with a girl. Using your left hand as I described above is a simple, kind gesture that will make you come across as genuinely interested in the girls you talk to. If you're meeting females for the first time in a business environment, though, I don't recommend putting the left hand on top of her hand during a handshake. It may not be appropriate. You don't want any girl to get the wrong impression of you.

After introductions, ask a girl about her friends, and whom she came to the bar with. You want to be a gentleman, so after a few moments of polite exchanges, feel free to ask, "May I join you?" You'll always have the option of offering to buy her a drink. Don't overwhelm her with the offer, but observe when her glass is getting low and act accordingly. If a girl has a drink that's almost full, you can say, "Let me get your next one." I wouldn't advise you to open a conversation with a drink offer, but it can work well during a more appropriate moment. The reason that it's not always the best idea to offer to buy a girl a drink right away is because you're sort of trapping her. Once a girl receives a free drink, she may feel obligated to talk to you for the duration of that drink at the bare minimum, even if she isn't the least bit interested in you. You're better off establishing some good conversation first, and then later play the "Can I buy you a drink?" card.

Use humor to your advantage. There's nothing

more powerful than being able to make a girl laugh and smile. Girls love guys who can make them laugh. Whether you're meeting a girl for the first time, on a second date, or in a relationship, having a good sense of humor is an important trait. There's a difference between spouting cheesy, cliché pick-up lines and making a joke to break the ice. First impressions carry a lot of weight, and if you make a girl laugh, this can't hurt your chances. Humor is the best way to keep the conversation light. Remember that you're in a social setting in which people want to laugh and have a good time, so don't always be formal in your approach and in conversation.

A few minutes into a conversation with a girl you just met, I suggest that you say, "You seem very nice. I hope that I'm not taking you away from your friends." At some point, compliment her, but keep it simple. Say something about her hair, dress, or nails. Don't overdo it with compliments, and avoid overly dramatic clichés, such as, "Has anyone ever told you that you have the most gorgeous eyes?" That is a total dork line, and it may take her out of her comfort zone.

When she introduces you to her friends, listen to them, and remember their names. Come on, guys, seriously, you can do it! Don't just think about what you're going to say next, but actually listen closely and respond to those around you. Pay attention. Ask her friends questions, and remember their answers, too. These are her friends. They are definitely deciding factors when it comes to whether or not this girl will ever talk to you again after tonight. As I said before, you have the option to offer to buy her friends drinks as well. Be observant. You should notice when one of her friends is without a drink, or if she has one in her hand that's nearly empty. This doesn't mean that you have to buy them drinks all night. Once is good enough, and it will go a long way. It's the gesture that matters the most.

So, what are the right and wrong topics to talk about with a girl who you've just met? Do not begin the conversation by asking her what she does for a living. She knows that you didn't walk up to her to ask about her goals and expectations in life. Also, do not inquire about family history. It's way too early for this. You cannot win with this line of questioning. Most likely, she realizes that you won't remember any of her family members' names.

What you do want to focus on is her name, her friends' names, and if she's having a good time. Once again, always be aware if she's rubbernecking. If she's not interested in you, a couple of signals should be evident. If she says she has to go to the restroom (either with or without her friends), especially if it's after you have asked her a question, there's a good chance that you should move on. You can also say, "Would you like me to wait here, or do you want to find me later?" This keeps her in her comfort zone and gives her options. This also benefits you greatly. After her answer, you'll know if you are wasting your time, energy, and money. If she opts for, "find you later," it's not automatically tragic news. It doesn't mean all your doors are closed. Even better, she might say, "Wait here, I'll be right back."

When she does come back, invite her and her friends to meet your friends, if you haven't done so already. She needs a wing-girl, too, and doesn't want to feel trapped with people she doesn't know. Always leave her with an escape route. For instance, at any point you can say, "Do you need to find your friends?" Another thing you should do is excuse yourself to go to the restroom. Even if you don't have to pee, go and wash your hands. Once you return, see if she's still waiting for you. This is another way to find out quickly whether or not the situation is a waste of time. I wouldn't run off to the bathroom two minutes into a conversation, but after a round of drinks or so is fine. It's a good strategy for you to step out for a moment.

If she's there when you return, it's a good sign that she's interested in seeing where the night might go with you. Continue to keep the conversation light. For example, ask: "Where are you from?" "Would you like to come to the bar so I can get a round for us?"

At this point, after you've shared a couple of drinks, it's okay to ask questions that require longer or more personal responses: "How long have you lived in this city/town?" If appropriate, "Do you have any family nearby?" These questions not only stimulate conversation, they help you get to know her better. Be aware of the environment around you, because it can be a source to help in the conversation. If a Journey song is playing, and you love Journey, ask her if she is into Journey. If she is, ask her what her favorite Journey song is, and so on. This is just one example of how you can use the environment to help make conversation.

Now, you might hear some good music playing in the background. Look to see if she's moving to the beat, if the rhythm is running through her body. If you are a capable dancer, this is an opportunity to ask, "I would like to continue this conversation on the dance floor, would you like to join me?" If she says, "Sounds good," lead the way with "Follow me." If the place is packed, it's okay to say, "If you need to hold on to my shoulder, please do. Either way, stay close." Keep her close, because there are plenty of other guys there hungry for an opportunity to get with her too, and if they sense that they have a shot, they'll take it.

Let's talk about dance floor etiquette. When entering any area where people are dancing, never approach a girl you don't know from behind. No touching, either! Don't go up to random girls and start grinding on them. That is not a good way to gain a girl's attention or a good way to initiate conversation with her. It might be fine if you're in college, where this type of behavior is more commonplace amongst those seeking one-night stands, but in the post-college world, I recommend being more of a gentleman.

If you want to use dancing as a way to meet somebody, dance near the person. However, I recommend that guys only do this if they are with their wing-girl or with a group of friends comprised of both guys and girls. I strongly recommend that you do not dance by yourself, unless you have skills like Justin Timberlake -- that's a different story. If you're with your wingman only, and the two of you are out on the dance floor together looking to meet girls, it's okay for both of you to dance, but you probably want to avoid dancing with each other.

So first, assess the environment. If the girl you're attracted to is on the dance floor and you want to approach her, make sure that she's not dancing with another guy. Go out there with your wingman, start doing some basic moves, and then quickly and smoothly head toward the group. Finally, and this goes without saying, you don't want to get caught dancing with your wingman for too long.

When you're dancing with your friend(s) near a cute girl you're interested in, face her and read the signs. If she turns away or heads toward her girlfriend, she's likely not interested. Whatever you do, do not follow or chase her around the premises. Let her be. If she comes back to you at some point, cool. If not, consider it her loss and move on to the next opportunity.

If she moves toward you, ask her to dance. "Is it okay if we dance for a little bit?" is a simple phrase you can use. Definitely ask her first; don't assume that she wants to dance with you. If you find yourself dancing with her, say hello and introduce yourself by telling her your name. If you have a wing-girl who enjoys dancing, this can be beneficial to you. It's much easier for girls to dance with one another and then introduce you. Use any available resources to your advantage.

Ends of songs make for good transitional moments and give you another opportunity to talk to her more. You can say something like, "Wanna get a drink?" or "Can I buy you another drink?"

One more thing about dancing -- I know that a lot of you guys out there aren't great dancers or aren't confident enough to dance in public, or perhaps you genuinely dislike dancing. Many guys claim, "I only dance when I'm drunk." What girls most want to see are guys who make an effort and show that they can have fun while dancing. Having said that, if you're not a great dancer (you know who you are!), keep in mind that "less is more." You want to move to the beat, but not make a complete fool of yourself. I'm reminded of the movie "Hitch," with a scene where Will Smith teaches Kevin James about dancing. Essentially, what he tells him is that less is more. Rather than trying to impress her with your moves (that are actually awful), you're better off bouncing steadily to the beat -- and not wildly flailing your arms. Search YouTube, "Hitch dance lesson." "This is where you live, right here... This is home..."

Guys, do not try to be cool by making it seem as if you could be with any girl in the room. If a beautiful girl walks by, do not make a comment about her and then say to the girl you're with, "but you're way hotter." Focus on the girl you're with, and only her. Once again, please avoid using cheesy lines. If she doesn't seem responsive, get out of there. Pay attention to the signs. If you're seeking a verbal response from a girl, just say, "I hope I'm not taking you away from your friends." Be careful with this line, though. You don't want ask every five minutes if you're taking her away from her friends and come across as a pushover.

If she says, "Oh no, no, no, you're not (taking her away from her friends)," then she's probably interested in you. If you get a response like "Yeah, I should probably get back," give her space. Perhaps you might have another opportunity later in the night. Don't be afraid to show patience and confidence. You can say to a girl in a moment like this, "No worries. I'll find you later and try to say goodbye before I leave." Although it depends on the situation, I wouldn't suggest asking for her number at this moment, especially if you've only spoken for five minutes or less. If you've been talking to her for ten to fifteen minutes or more and you feel like the conversation went well, then it might be okay to ask for her number. Just know that forcing the situation here could make you look desperate or come across as a guy who's only interested in a hookup.

You should almost never use your wingman to

"make moves" on your behalf. Don't use him to find out if she's interested in you or not. If you need things spelled out, do not have your wingman walk over to a girl and say, "So, my friend over there is interested in you and was wondering if he could buy you a drink." She'll think that you're not man enough do this for yourself. It's not a wingman's duty to make moves on your behalf; it's to keep up pleasant conversation and speak highly of you to girls.

Now, there are circumstances when a wingman can smoothly find out some crucial information about a girl you like, but you want to avoid coming across as immature and timid. This isn't high school, and you shouldn't have to use your friends to find out if a girl likes you or not.

As far as taking photographs, do not bust out the camera within the first few minutes of meeting a girl. Do not ask to take a picture of or with her. Wait at least until you've had a few drinks together and shared some good conversation before even considering taking out your camera. If you see that she has a camera, offer to take photos of her and her friends. If things seem to be progressing nicely and you two are connecting on some level, then it might be okay to try and get a picture with her. After snapping pictures of her and her girlfriends, you can say, "Could one of your friends take one of us, please?" She may even ask you to jump into a couple of shots anyway.

Do not ask one of her girlfriends to take a photo of the two of you right away. This could make the friend feel like a third wheel. If her girlfriend offers, you're fine, but I suggest you always take care of the girls first, before you take a photo of you and the girl you're interested in. Even better, ask a stranger to take a photograph of the group. This is usually the best option, because nobody feels left out.

Have fun, but don't be overly aggressive and creepy and take 700 photos. Always show her the photos immediately after taking them, and ask if she approves. "Is this picture good?" If she says it's not, tell her that you're going to delete the photo. If possible, bring the camera closer to her and show her that you're deleting it, then ask her, "Can we take another?" If she says no, respect her wishes. For guys out there awaiting an official rule for cameras, here it is -- you cannot take out your camera until she snaps the first photo of the night. If one of her girlfriends pulls out a camera and starts taking photos, it's now fair game for you to do the same if you feel the need to. If the night went really well and everyone's getting along and you and the girl are exchanging numbers, then it's probably okay for you to offer to take a group photo, especially if no one else in the group has shot any photos to that point.

If you've already taken a bunch of photos, you can ask a girl, "Would you like me to send you any of these pictures?" Depending on her response, this can get you an email address or even her digits, if you're lucky. Yes, this is a sly way to get a girl's contact information, and it's also a fairly good litmus test to gauge her interest in you. I mean, if you've been hanging out with a girl for some period of time throughout the evening, and you guys have already danced and photos were shot, don't you think it would be somewhat of a red flag if, after all that, she opts to not give you even so much as her email address?

To reiterate a crucial point, do your very best to

remember what she has talked about and the answers to the questions you've asked her. Remembering names is challenging. I, of all people, know how difficult this can be. If you repeat her name back to her when you first learn it, verbalizing it will help you remember it. It's also a nice personal touch. When talking to her, say phrases like, "Here's your drink, Mary Ann." Don't say her name every other sentence, though, because that's just weird. My point is that a girl might not be upset if you forget her name, but if you remember it she will be impressed.

Next to remembering her name, what's also challenging for me is to recall answers to simple questions that I've asked earlier in the night. Pay attention. This is a skill that can be developed over time. You do not want to repeat yourself, and you want to avoid asking the same questions multiple times. This can lead to her having doubts about you as a person, and whether or not you really care about what she's saying. She might think that you're only trying to get laid.

So, after spending most of the night with a girl (which perhaps included dancing, drinks, photos, and conversation), proceed to pull out your phone. I wouldn't suggest bringing up Facebook, email addresses, or the most ridiculous possibility -- her IM name. "Hey baby, what's your screen-name?" Avoid being ridiculous. You don't want to give her the impression that this is your first time pursuing a girl. Also, avoid scrambling at the end of the night in pathetic attempts to get phone numbers. If a girl you spent considerable time with earlier in the night sees you doing this, you'll come off like a douchebag, not a gentleman.

Do not ever offer a girl your number or ask her to call you. Unless it's clearly just a business or networking scenario, don't even think about handing a girl a business card. If she asks you for your number, instead of vice versa, the odds are not in your favor that she will call you. It's just her way of trying to be polite. A girl might say, "Oh, I don't give out my number." What this likely means is "I don't want to give it out to *you*." Give a girl your number if that's the only option that she's providing. There is a small chance that she will be in contact, but I wouldn't bet on it.

Continuing on the subject of "do not's," do not write your number down on a piece of paper; it will probably find its way into a trash can, if she doesn't lose the number first. C'mon people, we're well past the turn of the 21st century. Everyone has a cell phone.

So, when you decide that you want to ask a girl for her number, what are some simple approaches? Some possible phrases you can use toward the end of the night are: "I don't know how late we're going to be staying, but I would definitely like to talk outside of this environment and would love to get your number." Guys, it doesn't really matter how you ask for her number; she has probably already decided whether she is going to give it to you or not.

The most important thing to remember is that you should be bold. You want to avoid sitting in a taxicab on the way home with your buddies and thinking to yourself, "Shit, I should've asked that girl for her number." Above all, you want to avoid the "What if's" as much as possible. What's the worst-case scenario? She's says no. Big deal. Then, you're just at the same place where you started the night. You've lost nothing. If anything, you've gained more experience and confidence for the next time you ask a girl for her number.

When you do get a number from a girl, it's pretty much smooth sailing from there for the rest of the evening. Not that you should stress out about asking for a number, but all guys tend to feel more relaxed after finally obtaining it. After getting the number at the end of an evening, it's almost time to say good night and part ways. "It was a pleasure meeting you, and I'll get in touch with you this week." Go for the hug and the kiss on the cheek. Do not offer a handshake. A handshake is what business partners do in a formal environment, what we guys do with one another. Although it's unnecessary, you can ask, "Would it be alright if I gave you a goodbye hug?" As you're talking, extend your arms and turn your head very slightly to the side. This way, she knows you're not trying to make a move on her. Once she obliges, surprise her with a quick peck on the cheek. There should be no sudden movements or turns when going in for the hug or kiss, because you're easing your way in. Don't kiss her and then make a completely separate gesture to hug her. You want to go for the kiss on the cheek right as you wrap your arms around her, done simultaneously. This is the best way to avoid any awkwardness when saying good night.

Chapter 6: Other Than Bars?

You may have noticed that for the most part, what we've discussed so far is about approaching girls in bars. As I said before, most guys do not meet a potential serious girlfriend in such places, but these settings are perfect for fine-tuning your social skills.

I'm sure that you're wondering how to approach a girl in places other than bars. The concepts that I've shared with you can apply in many scenarios. Whether you're at the beach, the supermarket, on an airplane, or in line at Starbucks, be aware of your surroundings by scoping things out and doing your best to read any given situation correctly. Anytime you see an attractive girl, look for engagement rings and wedding bands. Also, take notice of who she's with and whether that person is a guy or girl. Pay attention to her body language.

Let me mention a few basic techniques that you can use the next time you're out food shopping. If you spot a girl in the meat or seafood section and she reaches for a package of shrimp, or something that you are knowledgeable about, crack a joke or make a suggestion about a recipe. "Oh, I love shrimp, as well. Have you ever tried them on the grill with lemon pepper?" Or, ask her how she likes to prepare shrimp. These are perfect segues to a conversation, and judging by her response, she will let you know if she's interested in you. If she talks about different ways of cooking shrimp, this at the very least indicates that she's a friendly person. If she is curt with you or doesn't maintain eye contact, these are not encouraging signs. If you suggest a recipe and she responds with, "Yeah, I've tried that before. Thank you," take note, because while she is responding to you, unfortunately she's also trying to end the conversation as quickly and as politely as possible.

A good way to start up conversation with a girl in the supermarket is by discussing items that you notice her checking out. If you see a girl holding an item while deep in thought, this could be an opportunity for you to offer your two cents. Be friendly and bold by stepping up and helping her out.

Listen to phone conversations around you. A girl could reveal something about her relationship status. This is an obvious example, but if you hear a girl say, "Honey, what kind of pasta did you want to make tonight?" then this girl is not single. I've continually stressed the importance of being aware of your environment. Remember -- it's one thing to be perceptive, but it's another thing to overdo it and come across as a stalker. You don't want to be caught staring at a girl too many times to the point where she is uncomfortable.

The fact that she's on the phone in the first place indicates that she's not interested in talking to anyone right now, let alone a stranger. Sometimes a girl might not be in the mood to talk to you. You need to take a hint, guys. It's nothing personal. Bad days happen to everyone, and she might be having one. If you spot a chick sporting a hat and she isn't picking her head up, she does not want to be bothered. It's perfectly fine to politely approach girls like this who seemingly want to be left alone. All I'm suggesting is that you be very aware of the reaction you might get, which probably won't be positive. Who knows if earlier in the day she had a big fight or even a tumultuous break-up? There's no way of knowing the entire history of a stranger just by looking at them.

As far as picking up a girl at the grocery store when you're in the checkout line, the odds of you being successful are minimal, at best. This is nearly the equivalent of trying to pick up a girl in an elevator. You only have a tiny window of opportunity to make something happen. This shouldn't discourage you from trying, but just be aware that in situations like these, there's a low success rate. But yes, it is still good practice for breaking the ice when talking to girls.

If you see a girl in the parking lot packing up her car with groceries, it's not a bad idea to go up to her and say, "I'm taking my cart back, would you like me to take yours as well?" While grabbing her cart, introduce yourself. Say to her, "I saw you inside. What's your name?" Don't be afraid to take chances and be spontaneous. You could meet somebody great just about anywhere, at anytime. Once again, initiating the conversation is half the battle. When you do have a conversation with a girl you've just met, remember to keep the conversation light. If you want to compliment her, don't overdo it by trying to be too dramatic. The goal is to keep a girl in her comfort zone.

Only try this cart technique if the moment presents itself. Life is all about moments. Ask yourself if life is presenting you with a good opportunity right now. These are the types of moments of which you ought to be taking advantage. If it's meant to be, it will be, but you must be the one to *carpe diem*, or "seize the day."

What you shouldn't do is sit in your car waiting for a girl. You also shouldn't loiter around the parking lot waiting for a girl, and definitely do not travel long distances across the parking lot to approach a girl who's loading up her trunk. There's no need to stoop to such levels of desperation.

* * *

"Don't shit where you eat." You may have heard this expression before. In this case, I am referring to getting involved with female coworkers. It doesn't matter if it's your boss, your assistant, or another colleague, you'll want to avoid crossing the line. What I mean is: nine times out of ten, if you end up hooking up in some capacity, it will end with someone getting hurt. Your reputation is at stake too. Mixing your personal and professional lives is a recipe for disaster. You can promise yourself that it'll only be casual by keeping feelings out of it, but we all know that sooner or later, either you or she will get attached, and the other person won't understand or feel the same way, leading to an uncomfortable work situation. If you're busy stressing out over this chick, eventually it will affect your job performance as well. You could be setting yourself up to get hurt financially by messing up your career, in addition to risking intense emotional distress on a daily basis. If you are quitting, about to move to another company, or your contract is up, getting together with a coworker might not be as risky. More importantly, it could lead to a more appropriate time to ask her out.

I realize that a significant percentage of married couples met one another in the workplace. It's understandable how and why this happens. People tend to spend most of their time around their coworkers, so it's natural that the workplace becomes a place where couples meet. Having said that, it's one thing to meet your future wife at work, but it's another thing to try to hook up with a cute coworker with whom you have absolutely nothing in common and no future together. If you decide to pursue a coworker, understand that there's a probability it will become a serious relationship right away, and there might be no turning back. Either you'll end up together, or you'll end up in an awkward situation in which one or both of you can no longer deal with being around the other person after a breakup or falling out.

From my personal experiences, I highly recommend not to shit where you eat. For instance, a company I used to work for hired a hot new receptionist. This is surely something that many of you guys can relate to. This girl and I (let's call her Dani) flirted for a while. It came very naturally to us, and there was definitely some attraction there. We continued our banter over instant messenger and through the occasional email. Time passed, possibly even a month or two of just harmless flirting. We finally hung out outside of work and our friendship became even tighter. Inevitably, after you spend this much time with somebody, when there is a mutual attraction the relationship becomes physical.

Just like everyone in this situation seems to do initially, we continued to pretend to be just friends. It was awkward, but considering the situation, Dani and I played it off pretty well until douchebag Toby, the I.T. intern, decided to check the history of my IM chat logs. He accessed records of private conversations that were flirtatious and of a sexual nature, learning how Dani and I coordinated our bathroom romance. It was the kind of scenario that sounds like something you see in movies or on TV.

What seemed to be rather harmless at the time proved to be a huge matter, when everybody at the company obtained a copy of my very private conversations with Dani. Douchebag Toby sent out a mass email of my private conversations to everyone.

After my secret was revealed to all of my co-workers, most of the guys high-fived me and most of the girls laughed it off, but that's not the point. The point is that my privacy was violated, and Dani's even more so.

Luckily, my supervisors and the executives were very forgiving. I also lucked out because my contract was about to expire, and I had no plans to continue working at the firm. If this were a job that I had planned on staying at for a significantly longer period of time, looking back, maybe I wouldn't have made the same decisions.

Even though I seemed to get away with all of this fairly unscathed, unfortunately for Dani, her life was affected in a much different way. She was embarrassed to walk around the office because sly comments were thrown her way. After a few weeks, she couldn't handle the environment any longer and she quit her job. I wasn't judged, but everybody around us viewed her as the company slut. It got to the point where she couldn't handle the jokes or the constant references to what happened between us. Even when no one said anything, she could tell what was on their minds just by how people were looking at her.

Thankfully to this day Dani and I are still friends. Luckily, she didn't hold any grudges against me, and she was great about sharing equal responsibility for what happened. However, it still sucks to know that douchebag Toby ruined her chances of becoming more successful with that company. The moral of the story is to be careful, and don't shit where you eat, because feelings get hurt and lives are disrupted. Even though I was lucky that time, I might not be so fortunate the next time, and the same goes for you too.

Another good lesson is to get rid of any paper trails that could come back to hurt you. Delete personal emails on work accounts and get rid of chat logs. Modern times call for modern precautions.

If you find yourself asking what other places or situations are off limits for meeting girls, there really aren't too many. For instance, if you live in an apartment complex or some type of community, weeks and months can go by without bumping into a girl you might prefer to avoid, meaning that even if it goes sour with a girl you dated in your building, you may not have to worry about awkward interactions, because these days even neighbors can go months without bumping into one another.

My advice to you is to go where you know there will be attractive girls. Increase your odds and put the percentages in your favor. It doesn't matter if it's the grocery store or a co-ed sports league, or even the bar and club scene for that matter. Be social and join groups and organizations where there are people who share your interests. Attend dinner parties and house parties when you're invited to them. Events that take place at the homes of friends, or even friends of friends, tend to be positive environments to meet new people. Unlike a bar or club, people tend to be less guarded in a private residence, making conversation less challenging to initiate. Put yourself out there and have fun. Seize any opportunity that presents itself to you at a moment's notice!

Chapter 7: Making Plans

You just had a fun night out with your wingman, wing-girl, or some good friends. You're now sitting in the car on your way home, and you and your buddies start to recap how the night went. At this time in the night, you might be feeling pretty good. In fact, there's a good chance that your B.A.C. is way over the legal limit. For you Puritans out there, B.A.C. stands for blood-alcohol concentration (or content). In my home state of California, .08 is the legal limit. It's a good idea to know your state laws, which can be found through a simple Google search. Most all of us (including myself) have made poor decisions, choosing to drive when we shouldn't have. Sadly, many people often drink and drive.

Not everyone who fails a breathalyzer test should be demonized. People have different limits. While drinking and driving is a dangerous reality, let's keep one thing in mind, though -- there is a difference between drinking and then driving, and drunk driving. Having a couple of drinks and then hopping behind the wheel is a relatively harmless act for many people. However, if you're slurring your speech, not seeing straight, and stumbling out of the bar, you should never drive, ever. Even if you have an amazing lawyer, an extra $10,000 lying around, and don't mind losing your driving privileges for a year, you still should not chance it. The worst aspect of drunk driving is that it not only puts you at risk, but innocent lives as well.

Regardless of potentially serious consequences,

human nature seems to encourage us to take risks, and that sometimes includes foolish ones. Just be smart, know your limits, and when possible, have a plan for how you'll get home at the end of the evening. Life's too short to be a dumbass. Your friends and family all care deeply about you, so get home safely!

Back in the cab, your cell phone is probably in your hands and you're staring at the name and phone number of the girl you just said goodnight to a few minutes ago. In your inebriated and possibly horny state, it may seem like a good idea to reach out to her, the perfect time to either text, or even worse, call her just to say something like "I had a good time, let's hang soon." Even worse and more risky is to try to reach out to her in an attempt to hook up that night. Think about it: you spent the whole night acting like a perfect gentleman, why ruin it by sending a text that gives her a completely wrong idea about you?

It's not a bad idea to send friendly and polite texts to a girl, but the timing in this case is off. Think about this for a second from her point of view, and also yours, if you are sober. You met a girl and this girl is somewhat interested in you, because you and she talked for a while and she gave you her phone number. You also shared physical contact in the form of a goodbye hug and maybe even a good night kiss on the cheek.

There's no need to rush into things. Take a step back and understand that you accomplished a lot, enough for now. It's a good idea to take some time between the initial meeting and when you next make contact. It's good to let her take in the whole night too, so she can reassess how she feels about you and how things went.

In situations like this, girls think differently than

guys. We know you want to pursue the girl by asking her out for dinner, coffee, or drinks, but I urge you to exhibit patience by waiting until you've obtained enough useful information about her (which we'll get into shortly) to be able to take her out on a real date.

You can send a short text message the next day stating something like: "I had a good time last night, it was nice to meet you." Do not send her a long paragraph describing your amazing time. If you choose to send her a message, all you can do is wait for her to respond. She may respond within a few hours, if not even sooner.

What do you do if she doesn't respond within a day or two to your initial text? You may ask yourself, "Should I try texting again? Should I call? If so, how long do I wait until another attempt should be made?" Even though nearly everyone text messages each other these days, believe it or not, there are actually some people who just aren't into this form of communication. Don't get upset if you don't receive promising responses from her right away. Even if you get no response at all, it isn't necessarily the be-all, end-all, but I must say that this isn't a promising sign, and the red flags can be seen from miles away.

However, don't give up hope just yet. She might not have an expansive text messaging plan for her phone and she could have gone over the limit for the month. Family emergencies or other extraordinary circumstances could have prevented her from responding to you in a timely manner. As mentioned above, there's also the small chance that she simply isn't into texting. She might prefer a call.

You want to know that you gave it your all, but at the same time, you want to avoid being seen as someone who's acting too desperately. If she doesn't text you back after your "It was nice meeting you last night" text, don't freak out and send more texts. I suggest that if you don't hear anything from her a day or two after your initial text, then it's okay to follow up with a phone call. More than likely she won't pick up, but leave a voicemail.

You must respect her wishes and her ways. Even in 2014, it's nice for a girl to receive a phone call from you. Every guy wants text responses ASAP from the girl he is pursuing, but that doesn't mean that she wants to get a hold of you at your convenience. Women are wired differently, and this fact often requires patience on our part.

If she responds fairly quickly to your first text within the next few hours, this means that she's at the very least curious about you, which grants you the green light to call her. She may not express this to you, but because you guys have been amicably texting, there is now an understanding that it's okay for you to take the next step and call her, if you choose to. In fact, there's a good chance that she wants you to call her.

When you do call, be a gentleman. When she answers, you ought to ask her, "Have I caught you at a bad time?" If you do catch her at a bad time and she says, "Yes, can I call you back?" This is a good indicator for you (depending on if she actually calls you back). Another option is to ask her when would be a better time for you to reach her. If she replies with something along the lines of "later tonight," or "tomorrow," she could be giving you the runaround, but you don't know that for sure yet. So just be cool, be patient, and see what happens in the next couple of days, but don't obsess about her by staring at your phone, eagerly awaiting her to hit you up.

If and when you do finally speak to her on the phone, have a real conversation. Do not ask her out on a date right away. Talk about the night the two of you met. If you didn't learn already, find out where she grew up. You can reiterate that it was nice meeting her the other night.

Ask basic questions that don't require her to open up entirely to you. For instance, ask her what she does for a living. Ask her about her hours and how long it takes her to get to work in the mornings. These are the types of questions that give you background information about her and will help you keep a steady conversation. This will also prepare you to talk about these subjects more in depth once you go out on that first date. "Do you live alone or do you have roommates?" This is another good question. All of this will help you set up a date, when you can have an easier time with more in-depth conversations. I call this "doing your homework."

Another universal subject is food. The reason that food is an important topic is because this information will help you later when you pick a nice restaurant for your first date. To be specific, go ahead and ask her if she likes seafood. If she says no to seafood, ask her if she's a vegetarian. Ask her what she had for dinner last night. If she says she had chicken, you can ask her if that is her favorite food. If she replies, "No, sushi is my favorite" and you love sushi too, suggest a place that you and she could go to. If you don't like sushi, say, "I like steak. My favorite is filet mignon. I also enjoy a nice porterhouse T-bone. What about you?" If she says that she enjoys steak, ask her how she likes it prepared. This is the kind of information that helps you get to know a girl better.

If you enjoy eating meat and she's a vegetarian or vegan, then you might be in a tricky spot. This is a bit of a red flag in my book. If you want to go on dates with a vegan and have separate meals that you'll never share, then go for it. Keep in mind that you want to get to the point where you can extend your fork and offer her a bite of your food. It's okay to have different tastes, but establishing some common ground will help you bond more with her at the dinner table.

* * *

Before jumping to conclusions about how you feel about a particular girl, you should feel out the situation a bit. Guys, I know in our sex-crazed minds this seems like a foreign concept, but don't be afraid to take some time to think about how you feel about her. Just because you met a girl and got her number, it doesn't mean that the two of you are going to live happily ever after. Don't jump to conclusions. This will save time, energy, money, and heartbreak! I promise you. I can't believe that I have to say this, but whether it's weekends or weekdays, don't ever call a girl you just met the next morning, or even before 1 p.m., just to play it safe. This is for you guys who have called a girl for the first time while she's sleeping. There's also something about texting a girl first thing in the morning that could come across as being overly eager.

It is important to get to know her better. This may sound strange, but believe it or not, you don't always have to ask a girl out on a date during your first phone conversation with her. By not asking her out during the first phone conversation, this may increase her level of intrigue in you. You'll come off the opposite of desperate. It may seem like the natural order to meet a girl, get her number, call her, and then immediately ask her out. Try talking to her. You might be pleasantly surprised by the results later on. There's also nothing wrong with saying something like "This week is kind of crazy for me to meet up... but maybe you'd be free to talk more later this week." I encourage guys to go for the second phone date before asking a girl out on an actual date. If you're really busy and genuinely don't have time to see her during the upcoming week, it's still nice to stay in touch with her, regardless, even if it's just a short chat on your way home from work. You want to let her know that you're interested, even if you haven't had time to ask her out on a real date yet.

It's also not wrong to ask a girl out the first time you talk to her. My goal is to let you know that you have other viable options, and you don't need to feel rushed, as if this first date needs to happen as soon as possible. If the conversation seems to be pointing in such a direction where it sounds like she wants you to ask her out, then by all means, go for it.

Keep in mind that she won't see you as timid for not asking her out right away. Think about it -- you had the courage to call her and converse in the first place. Not only will she be more curious about you because you've conversed without trying to get a quick date (or a roll in the sack), she may even become more attracted to you because you two had genuine conversation. She may see you as being even more of a gentleman.

Listen and pay attention to the conversation. If she uses phrases like, "We should totally kick it some time," then it sounds like a clear signal that you can go ahead and propose a specific time and date to get together. She might even come right out and say, "When do I get to see you again?" which is the best-case scenario.

When you finally confirm a date, you want to always try to pick her up. Inform her that you want to do this. Even if it is far, try to pick her up at her place and take her out somewhere that's closer to where she lives. Any place that requires a half hour to 45-minute drive would be about the furthest reasonable hike for a date. Typically you'll want to lead the way and pick a restaurant on your own, but there are exceptions when it's okay to get some input on where to take her -- like if you aren't familiar with the area. There's always Yelp, but either on the phone or in a text message, you can ask, "What's a really nice restaurant that you like to go to?" You can also try saying, "I don't know your area too well, and any recommendations for dinner are appreciated."

Because this is a first date, there a good chance that the two of you won't know each other very well, and she might be more comfortable meeting you somewhere, which is fine. You can say, "I'd really like to pick you up, but if you prefer to just meet up, that's cool too." Give her options, but also make it clear that you really want to pick her up, without being overly forceful of course.

Also, if you have a good idea of where you guys are going to head on your date, you might want to give her an idea of what to wear. I'm not only referring to proper attire in terms of jeans or a dress, but if dinner is going to be outside, for example, then she'll need to dress accordingly. It's not a bad idea to tell her to bring a sweater if you think one could be needed. If there's a good chance that some walking will be involved, tell her that heels might not be her best option. If you feel it's necessary, suggest that she bring another pair of shoes along. This might sound like a bit much, but it's just one more way to show her how considerate and thoughtful you are.

* * *

What do you do if you get her voicemail the first time you try calling? Leave a message. Say, "Hi, it's (your name here), from the (bar) the other night. It was nice to meet you. Just call me back when you can and we'll catch up." If you want, you can also briefly reference something that you guys discussed the night you met, or bring up something significant about that night. Was there something funny that occurred, or a moment that particularly stood out? If you choose to include an anecdote in your voicemail, this should go without saying, but make sure you refer to something you know with certainty that she'll remember too.

One time I met a girl named Lauren, who came to a barbecue with a friend of mine, and whom I had heard was a cute girl. Lauren and I were walking around together, then I sat down on a patio chair and she sat next to me. She put her feet up on my legs while we were talking, so obviously this girl was comfortable with me, and possibly romantically interested.

She asked me a few questions, and one of them was "Would you massage my feet?" I inspected her feet to see whether or not they were attractive, but also if they were clean. Low and behold, the bottoms of her feet were dirty and blackened from walking around the pool deck. I replied, "No way! Your feet are dirty!" She laughed, was mildly surprised, and was a little disappointed too! She looked at her feet after my comment and couldn't argue with my observation. You may think this is a bit inappropriate to point out a girl's dirty feet to her, but I have a point.

Let's fast forward to this hypothetical -- I'm on the phone with her for the first time. She will without question remember the moment when I called her out on her dirty feet. Now, while she might feel slightly embarrassed by this reminder, she also may be smiling and laughing on the other end of the line. You might want to say something like, "I still owe you a foot massage. I'm sure they're clean by now." This is the type of quick wit that also makes for appropriate texting banter.

You want to be able to envision a girl smiling on the other end of the line. Even though you can't actually see her, keeping her laughing and smiling during all of your interactions can only help you when you finally ask her out. If you can keep the fun and witty banter going without overdoing it, this will help your chances with most girls.

A popular theory among many guys is that to attract the attention of a girl, you have to insult her. Many guys think that you have to offend or even degrade a girl to break the ice. Or, guys tend to do the opposite. Almost every Tom, Dick, and Harry in a bar will go up to a girl and compliment her on her eyes, wardrobe or smile, and tell her how beautiful she looks. Ask yourself: "How can I stand out amongst such a crowd of unoriginal guys?" In my opinion, the best approach lies in a happy medium. You want to be able to playfully joke with a girl and even

97

make fun of her, but you'll want to avoid being too over the top or just plain mean.

Suppose that you are flirting and joking around with a girl you just met. Next, you crack a joke and she seems to take offense to it. Even if in your mind, you feel that you've done no wrong, apologize immediately. Keep in mind that this is a possible red flag and could indicate that her personality might be incompatible with yours. Whatever the case, it usually is good to diffuse tensions as quickly as possible, so consider saying phrases such as, "It was only a joke. I really didn't mean to offend you." Avoid arguing and unnecessary drama and confrontation.

Remember this, though, as well -- just because a girl is being friendly doesn't automatically mean that she's attracted to you. Believe me, it's not a stretch that sometimes girls will smile at you and laugh at your jokes just to be nice. Pay attention to the signs, and remember that behavior and actions carry more weight than words.

If you've left a voicemail and she doesn't call back by the following weekend -- which is one full week since you've met, then try calling again. If you get her voicemail again, do not ask to hang out in your message. Keep it light, and still sound like this is the first time that you're calling her. Keep it casual with a line like, "Hey (whatever her name), it's (your name), give me a call back when you get a chance, would like to chat with you." Short and simple does not reek of last chance desperation.

There are no hard and fast rules about when to text and when to call. But if you need a starting point, here are some simple guidelines that I like to follow -- three strikes and you're out:

-It's a next day text (after the night you've met)
-A phone call two or three days later
-Another call or text five to seven days after that.

I know what you may be thinking. You think that because she's ignored you twice, that you're being blown off. You're probably thinking to yourself, "I've reached out to her twice and have gotten nothing in return. I feel like I'm coming across as desperate to her." Maybe you even hear her voice in your head saying, "Can't this guy just take a hint?" True, she may have no interest in you, but you're not out of line by giving it one final shot. As we've previously discussed, you don't know what's going on in another person's life, and there could be a perfectly valid explanation for why you haven't heard back from her yet.

If these three "swings" are missed (no replies), unfortunately, you've struck out. That's when you are free to delete her number from your phone. Remember, it's her loss, not yours. We know what type of guy you are, and you deserve better treatment.

In the rare scenario where a girl who's number you've deleted finally decides to call or text you back, it means that you are presented with a good opportunity to ask her out. She's been giving you a bit of a runaround, so you're more than entitled to ask her out if you're still interested.

Suppose you leave a voicemail for a girl, and then she leaves you one while you're in the shower. Definitely call back right away. God forbid you get her voicemail again, but if so, leave another message, and don't be afraid to make it a funny one by acknowledging what is happening. "I guess we're playing phone-tag. You're it."

This sounds kind of corny, but she will think it's cute. Always keep phone-tag alive.

If you already have a girl's phone number, there's no reason for you to try to make plans with her through instant messaging or email. It's the 21st century, so there is nothing wrong with making plans through text. In fact, this is pretty much how things get done these days. Texting works. Keeping it simple is the crucial concept to remember about texting. This is especially true for the texting that will occur shortly after you meet a girl. Another important concept to remember is that a girl will always want you to be the one to send the last text of a back-and-forth texting interaction. She wants you to say the last words of a phone conversation too.

Here's a quick example of a common texting scenario:

GUY
hi! how was your day?

GIRL
was good, yours?

GUY
it was great...we should hang out some time this week.

GIRL
for sure ☺

Most guys would probably then reply with something like, "Cool, I'll give you a ring tomorrow." or right then and there try to make plans via text. Either is too much. It's overkill. So what should you do? Nothing.

Don't write anything back. That's how you keep her on her toes. You've turned the tables on her, and now she was the last one to say something and you've left her wondering, "Is he going to call or not?" Let her do the worrying for once. You're not being neglectful or rude toward her by not sending another text. You're just standing your ground. You always have the option to pick up the texting conversation later.

I recently met a girl named Amy at a graduation party. I was kind of on the fence about her because she seemed to always be busy traveling for work. However, I still wanted to see her again. After a couple of back and forth texts saying hello and asking each other how the others person's day was, I put it out there.

ME
Are you free tonight to grab some coffee?

AMY
Sounds great, but I'm pretty busy tonight. How about tomorrow?

ME
Sounds good. Pick you at 9?

AMY
Make it 9:30 :)

ME
Cool…address?

She texted her address, concluding this texting session. The next day, she texted me in the late afternoon:

AMY

I have a ton of work to do, just realized I probably won't be able to make it out tonight.

ME

No worries, we can just do it another time if it's too late for you.

AMY

I'll give you a call when I know what time I'll be getting off work. Hope you're having a good day.

Notice how she sent the final texts of those last two exchanges. Later on in the evening, she texted again:

AMY

Sorry babe, still stuck at the office…might have to reschedule for another night :(

Realizing that it's been kind of tough to coordinate schedules, and not wanting to throw in the towel just yet, I texted this in response:

ME

Would you want me to pick up coffee and just bring it to your place?

To my pleasant surprise, she replied:

AMY

Sure, I could do that…I'll let you know when I get home.

Later on, she texted me, telling me that she was home. I asked her what she wanted from Starbucks, and then told her that I'd be over in about 45 minutes.

As I was picking up the coffee, more texting:

AMY
Fyi, I'm in sweats and not changing…I'm too comfy.

ME
Good, I braught my pillow.

AMY
It's "brought" you dumbass JK :)

ME
I just spit in your drink!

AMY
Haha

Before you viciously make fun of my spelling skills and point out that I'm an author as well, understand that there's a reason why ghostwriters, copy editors, and proofreaders exist. The point of all this back and forth texting (while standing sadly in a long line at a coffee shop) was to make sure that I was always one up on her, in terms of playfully picking on each other, a.k.a. flirting. I'm giving you examples of how to use texting to your advantage. It's all about keeping it simple, and keeping her laughing and smiling along the way.

When it comes to phone conversations, the icing on the cake is for you to end the conversation first, and beat her to the punch. I realize that you don't always know how long phone conversations are going to last. What's most important is that you do not cut her off while she's talking, or end a conversation abruptly and awkwardly. Find a smooth transitional moment in the conversation during which to make an exit. When a phone conversation begins, you probably can gauge how long it is going to last. Some of you may be wondering what I mean by this. You can tell if the conversation is flowing in a positive direction by noticing how easy it is to talk to each other from the get go. You'll also notice if there are a lot of awkward silences, when getting her to respond to you is like pulling teeth. That's a good indicator that the conversation won't last very long. This is not the end of the world, just something that you should be aware of because it could be a red flag if it continues -- especially on a date.

Try to end conversations at appropriate moments, not in the middle of discussions. You never want to cut a girl off and tell her you have to go during the middle a story that she's telling you. At the same time, remember guys, you don't have to chat with her all night. There's no problem with saying to a girl at the right moment, in a polite manner, "I'm really sorry, but it's getting late, and I have a big meeting in the morning... Can I call you tomorrow?" Most likely, she will understand.

When a girl asks you how you are, whether it's on the phone, through a text or an instant message, don't be afraid to tell her that you're doing "great." Perhaps in actuality, you might only be "okay" or "fine," but you're much better off going with "great." Always be positive by presenting yourself as such -- especially at this early stage of dating. By saying that you're doing great, you give her the impression that you're an upbeat person, which most girls will gravitate toward.

She wants to feel that by contacting you, it has uplifted your day. Say you aren't having the best day. If you find yourself texting back and forth with a girl whom you're interested in, most likely this will lift your spirits. People vibe off one another. Even through texting, tone can sometimes be communicated. Be upbeat with your texts, because if you do, you're more likely to receive positive responses in return.

As much as I encourage you to be positive with your texts and to think about what you're texting and receiving via text, I strongly urge you to not over-analyze messages that you receive from girls. Often messages can come across in a completely different way than they were originally intended. Unless you know somebody really well, it can be difficult to decipher someone's mood and tone based on a text. If she sends you a short response and doesn't use smiley faces, it doesn't mean that she doesn't like you. On the flip-side, if she uses all sorts of exclamation points and smiley faces, it doesn't mean that she's in love with you either. Take her text messages with a grain of salt.

We all have had girls cancel on us either the night before, the day of, hours, or even worse, minutes before a date. Say she cancels some time during the day of your planned date. I'm going to give you some advice that will help you cope with this type of situation. It sucks, I know. However, let us step outside the box for a second and think this through. Isn't it possible that something came up that was more important? Again, you don't know what's going on in her life. Most likely at this point, you probably haven't seen her since the night the two of you met.

Nine times out of ten, guys will take the easy route. We'll think, "I guess that she's not interested." Guys tend to not give girls the benefit of the doubt by thinking and assuming that the girl really didn't have something more important to tend to. We often rush to judgment. Why? Over time, everybody develops his or her own habits and rules that he or she tends to stick with, no matter what the specific situation entails. While trapped in this box, we rarely consider what would happen if we stepped outside our box for once and saw more of the entire picture. With just a little patience and optimism, you never know what could happen.

Make rational decisions, because you never know if you're going to regret not trying harder with a particular girl. I luckily gave that benefit of the doubt to several girls, enabling me to experience relationships that I cherish to this day. If a girl cancels on you once, don't choose the easy way out and give up on her. I encourage you to do quite the opposite, and realize that it's crucial to not give up as easily as you may have in the past.

If it doesn't work out, at least you tried, and you won't have any reason to kick yourself later for not giving it your best shot. If you don't already know this from experience, believe me, any type of regret is one of the worst feelings that a guy can have.

I'm willing to go out on a limb and say you, the reader of this book, have experienced personal grief. Pinpoint that one girl you missed out on, when a real opportunity existed. Wondering about the "what ifs" or the "what could have been" will eat at you. Why put yourself through unnecessary distress? It can be avoided by taking what I've been talking about to heart.

Chapter 8: First Date

To briefly review what you've learned so far, I started out by giving you the basics leading up to dating, which is our foundation. You probably had not considered the importance of what leads up to a date. I've stressed the importance of taking care of your home and car. More importantly, I've reiterated the need to focus on taking care of you -- looking presentable as you're headed out the door. I even listed basic hygiene concepts that guys often foolishly neglect.

We've gone over the types of friends who you want accompanying you when you go out. I've touched on what you should expect from them. We discussed how you should treat your wingmen and/or wing-girls. I suggested how to approach women, as well as gave examples of what not to do when approaching them.

By now, you should feel good about yourself, and maybe even you've built up your level of confidence before your next first date. I can't guarantee that any date will be a successful one, but I've provided you the best opportunity to put yourself in a position to meet somebody you always thought you could never get. I'm referring to the girl you always thought to be out of your league and who you never had the courage to approach in the past.

* * *

It's Friday night, your car is clean, and you've just showered and gotten dressed. Your home meets an acceptable standard of living (in the mind of a girl). You hop into your freshly vacuumed and scented vehicle. You never want to show up late to pick up a girl, so be sure to give yourself some extra time. Before picking her up, you'll have to make a couple of stops. First thing that you'll want to do is get gas and cash.

Now, some may not agree with my next thought, but this is just one example why I am writing this book. I want to encourage more chivalry in today's world, because it seems that the whole idea is fading away. When I tell girls that I like to bring flowers on first dates, a common reaction is laughter. They'll often reply, "Wow. Who still does that? I almost never get flowers on dates." Girls will sometimes say to me something like, "I'd be a little weirded out if a guy brought me flowers on a first date." My response to this reaction is to tell her to envision a very attractive guy you like, bringing flowers for a first date. It changes her whole outlook. If a guy she doesn't like brings her flowers, she shouldn't be asking herself, "Why did he bring me flowers?" What she should be asking is, "Why am I going on this date with him the first place if I'm not even the least bit interested in him?"

So, pick up flowers for your date. Yes, guys, I said "flowers." For me, there are really only a couple of exceptions to this rule. The first situation would be if you were meeting a girl at the date location, not picking her up. The reason you might not want to bring flowers to a meet-up date is because it's not a formal date, and for some girls, flowers might come across as too formal or even too serious. The other reason is a logical one: she has no place to put the flowers during the date.

In most cases, though, giving a girl flowers at the

beginning of your date will show that you're secure in your masculinity and that you also have a soft side. Buying flowers is one more way to show a girl that you're confident and mature. It also establishes a nice tone for the night. Just so you know, you don't have to get her roses. Often, you can find beautiful seasonal flowers, just do not get red roses. To clarify, red roses signify love to a girl. Hey, love is awesome, but guys, if you're not looking to go all-in right away, you must realize that it's too early to bring out the red roses. It's easy to remember that red roses are a red flag to a girl on a first date. There's a very good chance that she'll even find a single red rose off-putting, but if you hand her a big bouquet of red roses, she'll likely be overwhelmed, and not in a good way.

If you do want to give her a rose, go ahead with a different color besides red. This might sound like a bit much for a first date, but if it's for a girl whom you're seriously interested in, then it's not misleading. Most likely she will be appreciative of your thoughtful gesture. What I advise is to stick to some sort of progression when it comes to buying a girl flowers. For a first date, it's tough to go wrong with any sort of flowers. For future dates with this girl, if you like, you can buy her different colored roses, and more of them. Try to use flowers to help express how you feel about this girl, and what you want. We'll talk more about this in the coming chapters, but if you're on your third date, for example, and want to take things to the next level, purchase flowers that reflect this. Even looking ahead past a third date, if you've made up your mind that you want to be exclusive with this girl and plan to tell her this, give her flowers earlier in the night; this will help set the tone for the evening.

There isn't a blueprint for when to buy what kind of flower, but you can use this information as a guideline. Generally speaking:

Red roses = *love and romance*
Pink roses = *elegance and beauty*
Yellow roses = *friendship (though not all the time)*
White roses = *innocence and purity, new beginnings*
Orange roses = *passion and desire*
Lavender roses = *enchantment*

If you don't know what to get, or even what to ask for when shopping for flowers, it's very easy to communicate this to a florist. Tell him/her that you don't want something too big or too fancy. Don't overdo it. Flower arrangements put together for you on the spot, as well as pre-made bouquets, are acceptable to present to a girl on a first date. Don't be afraid to tell the florist that the flowers are for a first date. It's their job to assist you in finding what suits your occasion best. It's not necessary, but it's nice to buy a vase too. This might sound like overkill, but think about what happens when you give a girl flowers without a vase. She has to cut the flowers and find something to put them in. A vase makes things a little easier for her. Depending on how interested you are in this girl and what your budget is, it's a judgment call when it comes to what flowers to buy and if a vase is necessary.

Before you go on your date, it's okay to think about some of the topics that might be good to talk about on your date. Don't over-analyze and stress by trying to plan the entire date in your head. Remember to relax, be confident, and most of all, have a good time. Don't go crazy and let a casual first date monopolize your thoughts and energy. She agreed to see you, so she must like you on some level. The date is going to happen. Why become stressed out to the point that it's distracting you from other aspects of your life? Why put yourself through unnecessary agony? It's counterproductive.

After you've gone to fill up your car with gas, taken out money, and bought flowers, you now have the option to send her a short text telling her that you're on your way. You don't have to do this, but it's a nice gesture and lets her know how much time she has before you arrive.

When pulling up to her place, call her (don't text) to let her know that you are outside. If she lives in a house, it's okay to knock on her door. If she lives in an apartment, call her using the building intercom or with your phone. If you call and she doesn't pick up, don't panic by continuously calling her. There's a very good chance that she's still getting ready and doesn't hear the phone over her hairdryer or bathroom fan. In cases like this, I suggest not leaving a voicemail or a text right after you hear her voicemail message. Trust me, she knows what tonight is.

Give her about five minutes, then send a polite text telling her that you are downstairs and that there's no rush. Most likely, though, while you're waiting for her, she's going to return your call either with a text or a call of her own within a few minutes. If you're looking for something to do while you're waiting in your car and you happen to have sweaty armpits (either from nerves or a recent hot shower, or both), now is a good time to turn up the AC in your vehicle to help dry your underarms. Another option is to roll down the windows and take a quick cruise around the block while she's still getting ready.

After you do speak to her, and she tells you how long it'll be before she's ready, then you know when you can walk to her door with the flowers in hand. Give her the flowers first, followed by a hug, and then a compliment. Tell her she looks nice and that you like her outfit. Everybody likes to be complimented, especially girls.

She'll either say, "Be right back," or there's a chance that she'll invite you in while she takes care of the flowers. If she invites you in, this is a good sign that she's comfortable enough to have you in her home. Being inside of her place gives you a sneak peek into how he takes care of herself and how she lives. This is an appropriate time to observe stuff that will help generate conversation on the date. Keep your eyes open for common interests. It could be the painting on the wall or that Yankees cap on her shelf.

When on a date, always walk her over to your car and open the door for her. Then carefully close it. If the two of you don't already have plans for a destination, you as the man should have at least two options for dinner. Never ask a girl when you pick her up, "Where do you wan to go?" She already has enough to worry about. Between her hair, outfit, makeup, and perfume options, she has a lot to take care of, and she's getting into a car with somebody she probably doesn't know that well. There's a good chance she's as nervous as you are!

It's sort of "old-school" thinking, but it should be the guy's responsibility to make the plans. This takes some of the pressure off her and makes her feel like she has a man who knows what he wants to do, and is prepared to show a girl a good time. Based on your previous texts and phone conversations, you should have acquired enough information about the types of foods that she enjoys. If a place requires a reservation, be sure to make one in advance. Do your homework and find a place(s) that will be easy for conversation. It's a wise idea to go to a restaurant that you know and have been to before. I do not suggest going to a movie. A first date should be more about conversation and getting to know one another. During a movie, you're not even allowed to talk.

You don't always have to let a girl know exactly where you are headed that night. Getting her to agree to dinner and a definite pick-up time is all you need to plan a date. When she asks, "Where are we headed?" be prepared with at least a couple of options. "I heard this place was pretty good." Remember, you don't want to make it seem like you have a particular place on lockdown, as if you go there all the time on dates. She wants to feel special and that her night with you is unique.

You might be asking yourself if it's always necessary to take a girl to a restaurant for a first date. Well, from pickup to drop-off, a typical date without an early ending or extended lifespan usually lasts about two to three hours. You don't want her to feel trapped, and you don't want to trap yourself! I like to suggest dinner for a first date, but if she suggests drinks instead, go with that. Once again, it comes back to keeping her in that all-important comfort zone. If she wants drinks, drinks it is. If you're nervous or not ready for an intimate dinner on a first date, and feel this is too formal, that's okay. Like I said, there are other options, such as meeting up for coffee or drinks.

Going out with a girl to places like amusement parks, or on hikes are totally acceptable, but they are not always the best ideas for first dates. The two of you barely know each other and shouldn't risk doing something that can easily become an all-day affair. If the two of you for whatever reason don't click, spending an extended period of time together could prove to be a miserable situation, so why chance that? If the two of you do end up spending more time together, let her do it of her own volition. Nobody wants to feel trapped by a situation. Dinner is structured to keep the girl's options open, so that she has at least some control over how long the night will last.

When you arrive at your dinner destination, if valet parking is more sensible than making her hike in her high heels, take advantage of the service available. After you park the car, get out and walk over to her. When she gets out, close the door for her. Something funny that I like to do is when I get out of the car, I lock the passenger side door with my remote. This locks her in so she can't open the door. I then walk over, open the door for her, and say, "I just wanted to get your door." If she already opened the door when you opened yours, and she's out of the car on her own, go over and close her passenger door for her -- that's if she or the valet haven't beaten you to it.

It's little gestures like these that girls will appreciate, find cute, and remember when they're describing the date to their girlfriends the next day. It's also sweet gestures like these that will make you stand out from the other guys she's dated in the past.

114

Many parking lots have bumps, steps, or other obstacles. If there is anything remotely dangerous around, offer your arm for her to hold onto. Do not grab her without asking. Just so we're clear, always get the door for a girl, whether it's car doors or doors to restaurants. This shows that you are a gentleman who's chivalrous and cares about this date.

Once you're inside the restaurant and about to sit down at a table, it's a nice gesture for you to pull out her chair before she sits down. It's not always necessary to do this; it depends on how much space there is behind her chair. If you have to contort your body to get behind her chair, just forget it. In this scenario, it's best to wait for her to sit down first, then follow suit.

The first thing that the waiter will ask is, "Would you two like to start off with something to drink?" I wouldn't suggest ordering a bottle of wine. Ask her, "Would you like a glass of wine?" If the waiter doesn't do so, you can also jump in and ask if she'd like a mixed drink, beer, or something else (with or without alcohol). If you order a bottle of wine on a first date, you could make her think that you're trying to get her drunk. Also you are driving, remember? So be responsible, and be cautious with the alcohol intake, especially on a first date.

Around the time that you order drinks, offer her some options and propose ideas for appetizers. Depending on where you take her and what foods you two enjoy (which you should know a little bit by now), you can take the initiative to suggest something like calamari. If she's not into seafood, bruschetta is a nice meatless option.

Take your time when you're ordering. Don't let

the waiter or the atmosphere make you feel rushed. Feel free to tell the waiter, "We'll start off with an appetizer, but we're in no rush to order." Other common and useful phrases you can use are, "We're still deciding," or "We need a few more minutes, thanks." This keeps the girl at ease.

When she's considering what to order, she might become intrigued by a couple of items on the menu. Once she makes her decision, you should consider ordering what she decided against. This way, you can offer her some of what her second choice was. Do not offer her a bite as soon as the food is served. After a few minutes of conversation, go ahead and ask her, "Would you like to try some of mine?" If you two are hitting it off and chemistry is evident, you can try to feed her using your own fork. If she politely refuses or comes toward your plate with her fork first, these could be indicators of how things are going. What a girl says over the course of a date carries weight, but it's her actions that will speak the truth about her feelings. Don't rule anything out just yet. Remember: she doesn't know you well and she might not be ready to share the same utensils yet. This is perfectly understandable. It's only your first date!

Remember to focus on her and look at her while you two are talking. As much as you want to check out her cleavage, keep eye contact! Don't rubberneck at other girls as they pass by, because this sends the wrong signals, especially if she catches you! Don't ask too many questions right away. The questions that you'll want to ask are ones that will require longer answers and stimulate conversation. For example, "What did you do today?" is better suited for the initial car ride. If something she mentioned during the ride is worth discussing in the restaurant, then by all means revisit that material.

Since you asked her out, you should almost never let a girl pay for anything on a first date. If the date is going poorly, then you can consider splitting the bill, should she present you with that offer. This is the only time when you can possibly accept any money from her. Be a gentleman by doing the right thing and almost always take care of the bill yourself.

What I consider a date gone poorly is a situation in which two people don't click. A bad date doesn't mean that the two people argued and fought. Whether it's breaks in the conversation peppered with awkward silences, an odd vibe, or constant disagreement, this is the exception to the rule and when it might be okay to split the bill. Even if romance isn't in the future for you and this girl, if she seems like a sweet person, picking up the tab is the gentlemanly thing to do. If it's obvious that she has no interest in you or that you have no interest in her, it's not going well. Who knows? There's a good chance that within the first five minutes of the date, you might be able to foresee where this is headed, whether it's going to lead to: a) a hook-up and nothing more, b) somebody who you likely will never see again, c) someone with promise, d) a potential friend.

As important as it is to keep a girl in her comfort zone, it is even more important to do so during the first date. Remember that the night you met her, she had escape routes. That's the difference between a first time meeting and a date. At the bar she can find her friends, she can get lost in the crowd, and she can easily leave and jump into a taxi. Whether she likes it or not, she's going to be stuck with you for at least a couple of hours on this date. Do the best that you can to make her feel comfortable, without being overbearing.

Do not answer your phone during a date. Make sure that it's either set to silent, vibrate, or off. Don't fiddle with it either. If you notice that your phone is continuously ringing or vibrating, it could be an emergency. If this happens, say to her, "Excuse me, I don't know what's going on, but my phone keeps ringing."

Once the plates are taken away, this is a good time to go to the bathroom. This is your opportunity to check your phone for texts, voicemails, missed calls, and any other non-emergency stuff (Facebook/checking sports scores). This is also a good time to see if you have anything lodged in your teeth. Everybody has that one tooth that always seems to catch food. Feel free to grab a toothpick off the podium near the hostess, or wherever the restaurant keeps them.

If you're having a problem with sweaty armpits, do not try to use an electric hand dryer to solve this issue. It will not work; it will only make you feel hotter and sweat more. All you can do is pat your underarms with a paper towel. Do your best, because it's your only option. If this is a persistent problem, you can buy a cotton armpit patch that can be sewn into your shirt. It will absorb the majority of your sweat and prevent stains in your armpit area. If you don't want to make the effort of having patches sewn into your shirts, there is a cheaper and quicker solution available -- disposable sweat pads. These adhesives stick in the armpits of your dress shirts and help absorb sweat. They are available in various stores that sell linens, such as Bed Bath & Beyond, as well as possibly at your local cleaners. These pads can be useful and are a popular item for celebrities who want to avoid visible, sweaty armpits on television. My friend, David, who's the head of the wardrobe department for the TV show "Dancing With The Stars" was the person who introduced me to this product.

* * *

When a girl gets up from the table to go to the restroom, you should rise out of your chair too. It's a sign of respect, and another way that you can treat her like a lady. By doing these certain acts, you're putting her on a pedestal. You're treating her like a date should be treated. You're not out to dinner with a buddy. Upon her return to the table, you should rise once again. Depending on the set-up of the table, it's also polite to help her get settled back into her seat. In addition to getting her chair for her, you should be on the lookout for other ways to show her that you're a gentleman. Not every guy thinks to do actions like these, but they are noble gestures that she will notice, remember, and appreciate. So be a gentleman, and go that extra mile. Too many guys don't consider gestures like these, which seem so basic, yet are very thoughtful.

You might be wondering what other good subjects are on a first date. Ask her some basic questions that will help you get to know her better. Casually ask her, "Are you a smoker?" If she says, "I'm not into cigarettes," and if you don't smoke either, then reply with "Yeah, it's like kissing an ashtray." If you guys are both smokers, then that opens the door for conversation about cigarettes.

Even though it sometimes seems that smokers tend to bond more rapidly than the rest of us, I personally feel that cigarette smoking is disgusting. Not only is the odor impossible to eliminate from your clothes, it's horrible for your skin, stains your teeth, and worst of all, cigarettes are proven killers. Anyway, whether you and she are smokers or not doesn't really matter. Ideally, you want to be on the same page, but if one of you smokes and the other doesn't, this shouldn't necessarily be an immediate deal breaker for you. In the end, you know yourself best and what you're able to tolerate.

When you ask a girl if she smokes and she answers, "What do you mean?", there's a good chance that she might be 420 savvy -- referring to marijuana. It's okay to tell her that you smoke too, but don't make it seem like you do it all the time. Just tell her it's "occasional." You want to convey to her that you are responsible. If she presses you on the subject, reiterate that it's no different for you than having a couple of glasses of wine.

It's not always best to go deep into conversations about weed, so you may want to move on to another subject. You don't ever want to talk about weed excessively on a first date. It's cool to discuss for a few minutes, but move on shortly thereafter to other subjects to show her that you're a well-rounded person, not just a stoner.

* * *

Don't dig too deep for skeletons. You should be careful when bringing up certain subjects. If you dig too deeply, be ready, because her answers might not be what you want to hear. You don't want to have unnecessary awkwardness or negative energy on your date. You also don't want to be too invasive with overly personal questions on a first date. The worst case scenario is bringing up a sore subject that will make her want to end the date and go home early.

Stay away from depressing subject matter, such as death, on first dates. I also urge you to stay away from controversial subjects such as religion, politics, or even sexual topics. These are subjects that people tend to have very strong feelings about. Don't ask her "for or against" type of questions. In other words, on a first date, it's probably not the best idea to ask for her stances on the death penalty or abortion!

Going down this road, you might reach a point where you two disagree. You don't want to be disagreeing with her too much during the date. You have the rest of your life to do that! That's why certain subjects don't make for the best fodder on first dates. You always want to try to keep it upbeat. Not to say that it's wrong to discuss taboo items, but you might want to avoid them, unless, of course, she brings them up first. If you're not entirely comfortable discussing certain subjects, that's perfectly normal. It's easier said than done, but guys, all you can do is try to smoothly change the subject.

Talking about past relationships on a first date is something you probably want to avoid. There's no reason for you to discuss your entire relationship history. If she does bring up exes, especially if she asks about yours, you might prefer to move onto another subject. If your date questions you about a girl from your past, you can always tell her, "It just didn't work it out." If you're being asked about a bad break-up, this is what you should respond with. If the break-up wasn't too traumatic, but there's a need to go into greater detail about it, you can respond with, "We broke up a few months ago, it just didn't work out." The reason you want to say the breakup was (at least) a couple of months ago is because the more recent the break-up, the more awkward the conversation becomes. Think about how she might feel if you tell her that you broke up with a girl two weeks ago, as opposed to a couple of months ago. If a girl finds out that she's your first date shortly after a breakup, there's a good chance that she will feel like: a) a rebound girl, b) you aren't ready to start dating again, and/or c) things aren't really over with your ex.

"It didn't work out" might sound like a cliché, but it's an honest response that she can't question. If it's true, saying that you're still on good terms with an ex is okay, but you want to reassure her that you've moved on. What's most important here is that the girl who you're on a date with feels secure in knowing that your last relationship is 100% over.

If a girl tells you that she recently saw an action (or typical guy) movie, don't prod to find who she was with that night. Even discussing the movie could bring her mind back to that guy. Keep her focused on you, and avoid the "I wonder what she was doing that night" type of thoughts. Why remind her of other guys? This date should be about you and her, not about exes and who you guys were hanging out with the other night. In any event, you should always focus on the present.

If you find yourself caught in a situation where she's going on about one of her exes, this could be a red flag, but be cool. Whether it's conversations about your exes or hers, if you want to move on, try to say something positive about the date you're currently on. Tell her something simple that articulates how glad you are to be with her. Go with something like: "Enough about exes, I'm just happy to be here with you, right now, so tell me more about yourself."

Ask her about her family. This will lead into questions like, "What do your parents do for a living?" Ask her about her siblings and if she's close to them, but avoid prying too much. If she speaks openly about her family, let her continue, and yes, listen to what she has to say and try your very best to remember as much as possible!

If she hasn't told you yet, ask her what she does for a living. If she told you already, ask her exactly what she does, to expand on what her work is like on a daily basis. Let her talk, don't interrupt. People love talking about themselves, especially females! Ask her if what she's currently doing is what she sees herself doing in the future. How a girl responds to this question will help you learn that much more about her. Is she a passionate person who has a clue about what she wants in life? Ask her about her goals and where she sees herself down the line. This shows a girl that you are serious about getting to know her.

If you find a moment when she stops talking for a second about herself (if you've got yourself a talker), it's okay to tell her more about yourself and your goals. I encourage this. Elaborate about your job and where you work. Talk about where you see yourself in the future. It's okay if you don't have definite answers to these kinds of questions. I'm letting you know that you ought to be prepared with responses, as opposed to winging it on the spot, which may make you come across as flustered.

Make sure to compliment her throughout the date, but pick your spots. For instance, tell her that she has nice eyes or has a beautiful smile. You can also say that you like her dress. If she's into you, she might compliment you back. "You look great tonight as well." Be careful; don't over-compliment. If you over-compliment, the words won't mean as much to her. We know that you want to say nice things about her, but if you overdo it, you could be hurting your chances by coming off as a player and not as a genuine person. Player or not, over-complimenting will make you come across as someone who's trying way too hard.

* * *

Let's say that the two of you are having a good time and enjoying each other's company. The date is going well, the conversation is flowing, and you're both laughing at the same jokes and stories. If the two of you finish the main course, go ahead and ask her if she wants dessert. You can present her with the option of sharing one. If she seems hesitant about dessert but appears she actually wants some, ask her, "If I get a dessert, will you at least have a bite?" If she says, "Sure," this could indicate whether she's interested in you or not, because dessert means more time with you. If the two of you split a dessert and you feel like the date is going superbly, go ahead, reach for the fork, and cut the first piece of cake, then extend your fork and try to feed it to her. We've already discussed what it might mean if a girl refuses to let you feed her. If she refuses to let you feed her with your fork, play it cool. Do not force the issue by leaving your fork extended for an awkward amount of time. If she doesn't want you to feed her, retract the fork nonchalantly and take a bite of whatever you're eating. Anytime a girl refuses to let you feed her, or refuses to try what you've ordered, I encourage guys to say something like, "Oh wow, this is really good. You sure you don't want any? You should at least try a little bit." Come off as playful and fun without being pushy.

If she says "No thanks" to dessert, this could indicate a few realities. She actually could be full, or she might want to end the date sooner rather than later. In addition to not ordering dessert, there are other simple signs that you can look out for that will tell you if a girl isn't feeling the date and wants to go home. Short responses to your questions could mean that a girl isn't into the conversation, or worse -- not into you. Remember that there are other possibilities here: she's very nervous, or is a shy person who takes her time before she opens up to others. You must also consider that she may just not be an interesting person and really doesn't have much to say.

Obviously, if a girl spends significant time texting and checking her phone, this isn't a good sign. If she tells you, "Listen, I'm sorry to cut this short, but I have to go help my friend out with something," this is definitely a red flag and a reason to be skeptical about her feelings toward you and the date. If you ever hear this line, nine times out of ten it is a lie, a way for her to get out of there. If she mentions that she has to get up early the next day or has something to take care of later that night, she's setting up for a possible early exit.

Some more about paying the bill: if you don't have the chance to ask the waiter for the bill and he sets it down on the table, and your date reaches for her wallet, grab the bill, look your date in the eye and say, "This is my treat to you. I invited you out." If she continues to offer to pay for some or all of the check, tell her, "Don't worry. I'll get it this time." This indicates to her that you want there to be a next time. One more time: a girl should almost never pay for anything on a first date. Guys, it should be at least two or three dates before you allow her to even think about using her money. You can't be cheap. Having a girlfriend requires funds; it's a fact of life. You want to be both chivalrous and generous in a relationship, but it's even more crucial to be on the ball from the outset with a new girl.

If things are progressing nicely, on the way back to the car you can say, "I really enjoyed this night and I don't want it to end, would you want to get some coffee or tea?" Ask her if she wants to grab a drink. Hopefully through conversation, you have found out if she enjoys alcoholic beverages. If she says that she has to go home or just isn't interested in prolonging the date, don't take it personally. Let her know that you're interested in seeing her again soon. "I would love to do this again some time" or "I had a really good time, hope you did too" are both simple lines that will give you revealing information. By using this approach and paying attention to her responses, you'll be able to better gauge how well things went. More importantly, this is a simple way that you can ask her out again without really asking her out.

If you did have another place in my mind to take her to, feel free to suggest it, but don't push too hard to continue the date. It'll turn her off and make you seem desperate, overbearing, or pushy.

Taking this all into consideration, should you

actually end up getting coffee with her, read the signs. At this point, you've invested at least a couple of hours with her, so she must be at least intrigued by you and by where things could possibly lead.

Once the two of you arrive at your next destination, look for new hints in her body language. Is her foot close to yours? Is she touching your arm a lot? Is she sitting much closer to you now than she was during dinner? Is she smiling consistently and laughing at your jokes? Her body language is almost always going to be more telling than the actual conversation you're having with her. I'm not saying that there shouldn't be a flow to your conversation, but it's how she acts that will give you a better indication of how she feels about you.

If you find yourself sitting closer, perhaps after a couple of glasses of wine at dinner, you might feel the urge to lean in and kiss her. Don't do it. Even if you're holding her hand, don't go to kiss her. You're supposed to be a gentleman and respect her. If she exhibits signs that she's interested, still treat her like a lady. If you jump at the very first possible opportunity to kiss her, you'll likely come off as too eager. You want to show her that you have the confidence that you're going to see her again, that you'll have more opportunities to make your move.

At some point during this date, you will likely come to realize whether or not you want to see this girl again. Once you come to the conclusion that you do want to go out with her again, don't force the issue of getting together. Never bring it up more than once during a conversation at some point in the night, then again at the end of the night. Attempts to make future plans more than twice during the course of a first date is pushing too hard. Every time that she mentions a common interest, you don't have to jump on board right away and say something like, "We should totally do that sometime!" It's okay if you say something like this a couple of times during the date, but don't make it sound like you're overly eager to hang out. Girls will see this as too needy and impatient.

At the end of the evening when you drop her off, open the car door and tell her, "I really enjoyed this date. I hope that we can do it again soon." This will get you more feedback. Tell her "Have a good night," extend your arms, and say, "All right, give me a hug, (insert her name)." Depending on the time of night that you're dropping her off, you could also say, "Sweet dreams" or "Sleep tight." During the hug, kiss her on the cheek. To review, this is how it's done -- when you go in for the hug and your arms are around each other, you'll feel her cheek against your cheek. This is when you make that subtle and smooth turn and plant one on her cheek. Do not pull back and kiss her on the lips. Look her in the eyes and say, "Thanks again for a great night." Go with this line after the hug.

If there's no place to park, and if the situation doesn't allow you to walk her to her door, right before she goes inside her place, she'll likely turn around and wave. Roll your window down, wave, and say goodnight. Do not drive off until you see that she's safely in her home.

Before you part, it's not a bad idea to make it clear that you want to see her again. You're likely going to set up plans for the next date sometime within a few days, at the most. I encourage you to play it cool by not attempting to make specific plans with her right at the end of your first date with her. You don't need to ask, "Are you free this Thursday at 8 p.m.?" It's okay to suggest meeting "sometime to do something." Be careful with your words, and don't pressure her too much. Be sure to give her space, and of course keep her in her comfort zone! It's never a bad idea to sleep on things. Sometimes we get caught up in the moment, and we're unable to see the whole picture.

I wouldn't recommend going for a kiss on the lips or making out on a first date. Don't assume anything. Even if she's being very flirtatious and appears to be into you, don't expect that she's ready to have that first kiss just yet. If things seem to be progressing nicely, relax; you will have another opportunity soon.

Having said this, I don't want you to feel that no kiss on the first date is a rule that's set in stone. If the situation feels right and all signs are pointing toward a kiss, then by all means go for it. You may think that asking for a kiss is a bit weak, but I'm serious about bringing back old-school chivalry. Some girls might prefer you to just know when they want to be kissed; others prefer otherwise. When it comes to asking, a possible approach is to say something like, "I had a great time, and I was wondering if I could give you a goodnight kiss." If she gives you the go-ahead, then go for it!

The flipside is if she does not want you to kiss her. She'll most likely tell you (hopefully in a polite way) that she doesn't kiss on a first date. If a girl tells you this, it doesn't necessarily mean that she's isn't interested in you. By wanting to take things slow, she's protecting herself and her heart until she finds out if you are for real, and potential boyfriend material.

Chapter 9: Second Date

Some time ago, I had a first date with Julie, a rather attractive Pilates instructor. The date consisted of dinner and then coffee. It seemed to go well. As the night wrapped up, I leaned in for a goodnight hug and kiss on the cheek in front of her apartment building.

I texted her the next day:

ME
Had a great time last night, thanks again. Hope you're having a good day.

JULIE
I did!...Thanks, you too.

Girls typically keep their texts very concise. We guys have a tendency to write novels. There's nothing more frustrating than agonizing over trying to figure out the perfect text, then sending it, only to receive a response with five words or less in it. Guys, you know what I'm talking about. And girls out there reading this, I'm going let you in on something: guys just want a girl to respond and actually ask a question when texting back, anything to keep the text conversation going a little bit longer. We want something open-ended that shows that you're at least a little interested in what we have to say, and not playing games. Something as basic as asking us how our day is going is all we really want in return.

Even though you might like to get a text

conversation going with a girl and don't mind sending long texts back and forth, you're much better off keeping your texts short, just like she does. The more efficient and effective you are with your texting, the more you'll come across to her as being relaxed and cool. You don't want to bombard her with lengthy texts that ask a million questions.

An important part of the second date is obviously making plans for it. Hopefully you'll be even more comfortable when planning the second date. By now, you've already spent some time around her. You might not know her well, but she's no longer a complete stranger.

If you enjoyed the time you guys spent together (which obviously you did, since you want another date), think back and recall some of the topics that you discussed, perhaps even at length. Rehashing old material is an efficient way to get off to a good start on the next date, but be careful. You don't want to ask her the same questions over and over again, forcing her to repeat herself. This will only expose you as the type who doesn't listen, and if you don't listen, then she'll think that you don't care about her or what she has to say.

If you traveled a considerable distance for a first date with a girl, it's okay to give her the opportunity to make the trip closer to where you live this time. In fact, she might offer to come to you, or perhaps offer to meet you halfway. Regardless, you should always make the offer as the potential traveler. It's courtesy, and it will bring out the part of a girl who desires an old-school kind of guy, willing to make the extra effort to see her.

* * *

Here's another tidbit for you on what you should not say to a girl, which applies to texting, phone, in person, or any other form of communication. Don't ever say to a girl at any point, "I was thinking about calling you yesterday, but…" It doesn't matter whether something came up, you forgot to call, or you were nervous about what to say to her, so you put off reaching out. Whatever the case may be, telling a girl, "I meant to call you," makes you seem full of excuses. You won't seem confident, and you might come across as someone who is not man enough to call her on the phone. Also, she could get idea that you're flaky and unreliable, or that you have other girls on the radar. This could be a potential turn-off. Don't be hesitant. Man up. Go for it.

For a second date, you have more options in terms of where you guys can go. No longer are activities such as going to movie theaters and amusement parks off-limits -- provided that it's been established that both of you share these interests. Going out to dinner once again is always a safe choice, but this time perhaps you'll want to take her to a more romantic place. Take her somewhere that has nice ambiance, preferably somewhere dimly lit, mostly by candlelight. Remember, it's not Valentine's Day, a birthday or an anniversary, so don't go crazy by spending lots of money. Just be sure to take her somewhere different than on the first date, and probably to a place that serves a different cuisine.

I don't always like to tell a girl where we're going on our date. When she asks where I'm taking her, I like to say, "It's a surprise. Is that okay?" It's nice to surprise a girl. They then have something to look forward to. It's all about the anticipation, especially for girls. What girl doesn't enjoy fun surprises? This concept can really apply to any date -- first, second, third, etc. Girls don't always need to know exactly where you are headed on your dates. You're building trust here. Think about it. You're now on a second date with her, so she's probably comfortable enough with you to handle some surprises.

However, don't use this "surprise dinner location" tactic too often. It will lose its charm. Use your best judgment and pick your spots wisely. Shortly after you've met a girl and developed some chemistry with her, she'll be more comfortable with you. But beware: if you find yourself in the midst of an awkward struggle, meaning things in general with her haven't gone exactly how you envisioned so far, then the surprise dinner location might come across as a creepy gesture. Quite simply, you probably haven't earned her trust enough at this point.

When picking up a girl for any date, always go for the hug when you first see her. Don't hesitate. It will make the situation awkward if you do. Be confident when you go in for the hug. Although it's not a requirement, I suggest not forgetting the kiss on the cheek either! And once again, never, ever go for a handshake.

Once again, when you're out on the date, don't give her too many compliments. She will be overwhelmed. Point out the little things that she's put work into, like her hair, nails, or her wardrobe. Even if you actually think that her dress is ugly, tell her you like it anyway. It's always best to keep it simple. "Wow, you look great. I love your dress." You don't have to give her a full fashion critique.

Perhaps the most important aspect of the second date is that this is when you are maybe starting to recognize if there's any potential with this girl. If you're like me, between the ages of twenty-five and forty, you are beginning to evolve as the years pass. I'm not trying to scare you, but on some level I would guess that you're looking for the girl you are going to marry someday -- whether you know it or not.

Dating, finding, and then staying with the right person is way easier said than done. Everyone makes mistakes on their journey. That's just life. Deep down, we know someone is wrong for us, but sometimes we can't help it, and we pursue what isn't always best for us in the long term. We all make regrettable decisions, whether it's a one-night stand, a bootie call, or my personal favorite -- calling up the ex!

I'm not here to judge anyone. Believe me, I can empathize with many situations. I just want you to learn from your experiences, good or bad. As long as you grow from them, then it's never for nothing. Every experience that you go through in life can only benefit you as a maturing individual that you should strive to become.

* * *

Hopefully you've paid enough attention on the first date to make smart decisions for the second one. From your previous interactions with her, you'll have a good sense of her general likes and dislikes. Take advantage of the knowledge you've obtained. I can't reiterate enough how important it is to pay attention to the things that she says throughout your time together.

At the beginning of the second date, you still want

to give her some space at the table while you guys are eating. Gradually, if the conversation is going smoothly and you both seem to be having a good time, then you have the option of moving closer to her. If you are both laughing and flirting, you can say something in humor such as, "Why are you sitting so far away? Do I smell?" If she replies with, "I don't know, this is just where I sat," or another vague response, then ask her, "Can I move a little bit closer so I can hear you better?" If she responds with "Sure," then take that as a sign to move closer to her. If she responds with, "No thanks, you're okay," this is definitely a red flag and a sign that she might not be into you. However, don't rule out that she's just shy and wants to take things at a slower pace than what you might be used to.

It's incredibly important to learn how to go about reading these potentials signs -- in terms of what she's saying, but more importantly in her body language and behavior. It's always good if she's smiling and laughing at your jokes, but it's even better if she's flirtatiously touching you at the same time. Whether she touches your shoulder, hand, or thigh, it's positive. If she touches your shoulder while uttering, "Oh, that was so funny," or if she excitedly reaches for your thigh and says, "Now I remember what I wanted to tell you!" -- this type of physical contact is her way of showing you that she's become more comfortable with you, and is probably becoming more intrigued, and attracted to you too.

Not that you shouldn't ever initiate physical contact with a girl during a date, but in my opinion it's a better approach for you to let her initiate the physical contact. After she gives you a couple of playful touches, you're probably okay to reciprocate from here on out.

Remember, though, don't go overboard and start touching her after every other sentence.

Before I talk about holding hands and how to go about doing so, I want to make sure that you guys know that you have another, significantly less bold option. This is something that you can do early on your second date or even on your first. What I'm referring to is (while walking together) extending your arm, elbow out, so she can either grab onto your arm with her hand or wrap her arm around yours. Either way, you're being a gentleman, and you're showing her that you're confident by initiating physical contact.

If you want to hold her hand, I suggest asking her while walking to the car (and not inside of the restaurant), "Would it be okay if I held your hand?" If you don't feel completely comfortable asking that but want to hold her hand, try easing into it by simply, yet enthusiastically letting her know that you had a good time. Being positive and excited is a plus, but please don't overdo it and go all Tom Cruise jumping on Oprah's couch either.

Should you be lucky enough for her to say "Yes" as she moves her hand closer to yours, I suggest going for interlocked fingers, not for a palm-to-palm grip. Interlocking fingers is a simple and subtle way for you to communicate to her that you like her. Palm to palm is for helping little kids cross the street. It's not terrible to do palm to palm, but interlocking fingers is more of a sign of intimacy. It is one more way to show her that you're interested in her.

While the two of you are headed to the car, smiling and holding hands, I should note that it typically isn't the best idea to try to hold hands on a first date. In most cases, the second date is the earliest opportunity to hold hands. If you met someone at a party over the weekend, texted a bit, and then went out on a date the following week, holding hands would most likely not be appropriate because it will be way too soon. On the other hand, if you've known someone for a while, even as a friend, and you're finally going out on a first date, then holding hands could be a possibility.

It's imperative that you use your best judgment and try to read what she's feeling, if she's ready for you to make a move to hold her hand. I want to encourage you to be bold, and if you sense an opportunity, go for holding hands on a first date. Needless to say, throughout the time you two spend together, she's going to be on the lookout for the little signals that you're sending her way, and wanting to hold her hand is a strong one. If she doesn't seem comfortable or ready to hold hands just yet, you're better off taking things more slowly. Holding hands can be very intimate for some people, so there are no hard and fast rules of how many dates you must have before holding hands. What's most important is keeping her in her comfort zone!

Once you return to the car, holding hands doesn't need to stop. As long as you can drive with one hand, you're fine. At anytime during the car ride, just extend your arm out toward her hand. If she holds it, that's great. If she creates a diversion by going for her purse, this is another potential red flag. Don't be too deterred by this, though. Just continue to act casually and enjoy yourself.

After pulling up to her place and the car is in park, it's a good time to tell her (if you haven't already), "I had a really good night." She will likely respond with something similar. Wait a second or two, and if she doesn't invite you in, then offer to walk her to her door. The most convenient moments for the first kiss are when you're saying good night and goodbye in the car, or at her door. You can ask for the kiss as you're hugging her and giving a peck on the cheek goodbye. Whether it's in the car or at her door, you'll want to look her in the eyes (eye contact is always key) and say, "I was wondering if I could give you a good night kiss…" Another cute little question you can ask is, "May I give you a little kiss on the lips?"

Sometimes it's more obvious if a girl wants you to kiss her, so of course it's not always necessary to ask. Some good indicators are if your eyes are locked, she's smiling from ear to ear, you're holding hands tightly, or if she's leaning closer and closer to you. If she has both arms wrapped around you and is gazing up at you, it's pretty obvious that she wants you to kiss her. If she seems very slow to get out of your car, and both of you seem to be prolonging the goodbye, more often than not, the girl is waiting for you to make the first move.

So, after much anticipation, you finally kiss her for the first time! Afterward, sometimes it's nice to compliment her kissing ability. You can mention her soft lips or even say something bold like, "Wow, just how I imagined it -- amazing." A quick little line can help break any tension or awkward silences for those few seconds following your first kiss. After you compliment her, it's always nice to hear something positive in return like, "Wow, that was nice." Remember that actions speak louder than words, so words might not be necessary at all. If the kiss was clearly pleasant for both of you, then keep kissing her!

Keep in mind that if you don't kiss well together, it

could be a sign that the romance isn't there, for whatever reason. Believe me, there's a good chance that she's going to feel the same way. Don't give up so easily! Relationships take work and time to grow. If both of you seem aware that the kiss didn't go too great, this is not a cause for alarm. First kisses often don't go 100 percent smoothly. It's nobody's fault. Nerves kick in, and the two of you are feeling at least somewhat self-conscious. Why should it be expected that everything go perfectly? It's only the first kiss! If the kiss ends and shortly thereafter she says goodnight, it's clear that a kiss is all you're going to experience for the evening. As on the first date, wait until she's inside her place safely, then wave and head off on your way.

Let's say that you're on a date with a girl who seems to be very polite and sincere. She smiles and says something like "Aww, that's sweet of you, but I don't usually do that on a second date," (in response to you asking for a kiss.) If a girl tells you this, as I mentioned at the end of the last chapter, it doesn't necessarily mean that she isn't interested in you. Be patient, and avoid coming across as too eager.

An obvious example of a girl who is not interested in you is if you ask for a kiss, and she responds with, "I don't know if there's anything here." Sorry, guys, if you hear a line like this, it's not going to happen. I advise you to play it cool and be polite. You could respond with, "I had a really good night, thank you. Let's stay in touch." That's about all you can say in terms of trying to make future plans with the girl. C'mon, guys, if a girl tells you right to your face something like, "I don't think there's anything beyond a friendship here," don't push for another date with her. Avoid the common lingo like, "So when do I get to see you again?" or "What are you up to this weekend?" The two of you may end up hanging out again eventually, as friends, but it's probably best to give that some time. In a situation like this, it's ideal that both parties know that they are going to move on after this date.

If this happens to you, it's definitely time to start over. You shouldn't feel devastated or down on yourself. To be quite blunt, beating yourself up over what's happened is a complete waste of time and energy. You know and I know you can and will do better soon enough. There's no point in overanalyzing the events, constantly trying to recall the moments when things might've gone wrong. More often than not, when things don't work out between two people, it's nobody's fault, and it's most likely for the best anyway. So please, do not think that you've failed because of the things you said or did. Do not think to yourself, "Wow. I bought her flowers and dinner. Not to mention I was a complete gentleman to her throughout both dates." Just because you made the effort and even followed my advice closely, there are still no guarantees. Remember, connections are built on chemistry and feelings, not magical formulas.

If two people aren't compatible, there's no sense in forcing the issue, because down the line, both of you will get hurt and may come to realize that you've wasted each other's time. "Wasting each other's time" may come across as a harsh reality, so you want to learn from your mistakes to avoid making the same ones over and over again. For example, by putting yourself through drama with the wrong person, at least you'll learn more about what you don't want in life, as you pursue what you do want and what's right for you. This is the healthiest mentality a guy can have when a girl rejects him, or when a situation with a girl just doesn't work out.

Now that you have those first and second dates under your belt, suppose you don't want to pursue anything further with this girl. You don't need to justify why you're not interested in this girl romantically. The fact is, at this point, you've come to the conclusion that you don't have feelings for her. It could be something with the chemistry, and that's okay. You gave it an effort, and hopefully at the very least you had an enjoyable time with a cool person, and maybe even learned something from the experience. By going on dates, even ones that don't seem to develop into anything significant, you'll find that your confidence will increase. We're learning about ourselves, and what our own personal "do's and don'ts" are when it comes to dating.

Now let's backtrack for a moment. Let's say that you've just gone on at least a first date with a girl. For whatever reason, you have absolutely no desire to go on another date with this person. By the end of the first date, maybe you've reached a decision in terms of whether or not you want a second date. Sometime during the goodbye, possibly the last words from you to her could have been, "I'll be in touch." For the handful of women reading this, note the difference when a guy tells you, "I want to see you again. What's your scheduling looking like this week?" and "I'll be in touch." If a guy wants to see you again, he'll attempt to make concrete plans with you sooner rather than later.

Unfortunately, both guys and girls can get hurt. That's just life. Everybody gets rejected at one point or another. Girls, just go grab your preferred chocolates, pop in your favorite 80's flick ("Dirty Dancing") and don't forget that bottle of wine! Then the next morning, start fresh and move on with your chin up. Sorry to be so blunt, but seriously, you and I both know in the long run that moving on is for the best. It's okay to feel bad for a little while after a disappointment with a guy, that's normal and expected, but don't beat yourself up over it, especially if you only went on a few dates with him.

Guys, if you decide that you don't want to have anything to do with a girl, not even being a friend, that's okay. It's not wrong to completely cut people out of your life. You have no obligations at this point to somebody you've only gone out with on a couple of casual dates.

Yet, it's often foolish to dismiss an opportunity to be friends with a girl for a few reasons. For one, think about all of the female friends she must have whom you haven't yet met. If you terminate a friendship preemptively, you'll never find out if she has any hot friends! You might be thinking to yourself, "I can't go out with one girl, end things with her, and then try to date one of her friends I might like more. Won't things be weird? Wouldn't there be jealousy?" Perhaps, but remember, you only went out with this girl a couple of times. Assuming you treated her very well, with respect, and never made any false promises, she's that much more likely to be cool with the situation, and maybe even help you out as a friend and a wing-girl.

We've already established the qualities that an effective wing-girl possesses, so why not always be on the lookout for such a person? Whether you already have a wing-girl, want another, or are looking to get your first, be smart and make friends. I suggest that you make a note of girls you click with on a level other than romantically. Trust yourself and your choices of girls you feel most comfortable with as your friend.

In every dating scenario that doesn't work out, and in every relationship that doesn't work out, no matter the reason, one person will always feel more rejected. It sucks for anyone to get rejected, but it happens to everyone. Just be honest with yourself, stay positive and keep meeting new people. Move on with your life and don't ever feel like you're taking steps back. Use your experiences as the building blocks to becoming the person you truly want to be.

But, if after your second date (which seemed to go well), you find yourself driving off alone instead of being in her bedroom, try to exercise some patience. Relax, be cool, and take a breather. Take a broad view at what you've accomplished so far. She's still showing interest in you, she hasn't left her comfort zone, and you have a great opportunity. A third date is looming.

Chapter 10: Third Date

You've just dropped your date off at her place and now you're headed home, recapping the night in your head. You might be creating a rough list in your mind of what went well and the rough patches during your latest date. You recall the moments when you guys shared laughs and enjoyed the same jokes. You think about basic stuff that you have in common (taste in movies, music, other hobbies, sports, etc.). As a guy, you'll no doubt also be remembering her nice eyes, nice legs -- whatever it is about her physical appearance that you find attractive. In addition to her physical attributes, don't neglect the chemistry and overall effect that her personality had on you. Was she funny, smart, and easy to talk to? Did she exude warmth and make you feel comfortable?

You'll also recall the times during the date when you thought you made mistakes, or where there were awkward moments. If you regret something that's correctable, you'll know to not make the same mistake twice. Ask yourself if the conversation flowed, or if you seemed to be talking over each other. Were there any long, awkward silences? Unfortunately, there are many things that can go wrong at any point during a date.

Even if you think that your date might not have gone so well, don't be discouraged. If you're feeling unsure about how things went, it's best to focus on the positives. When you get home, take your shoes off and relax. Soon after, you'll find your phone in your hands, staring at her name and thinking about texting her. Go for it. Text, "(her name), I had a wonderful time. Just wanted to say goodnight. Talk soon." What I often like to do is send a "next day text" after a first date, and a "same night text" after a second date.

Like I mentioned earlier for the most part (especially in the early stages of dating someone), you never want to ask a girl to call you. At the end of a date, never say, "Give me a ring sometime." Also, you should never text a girl asking her to call you. Of course, if you call a girl and she happens to be busy at that moment, it's okay to say something like, "I can give you a call later, or if it's more convenient for you, just give me a ring when you get off work."

Part of being chivalrous is taking the lead and wearing the boots. I want you to be confident enough to take the initiative to call her to set up dates and times. Do so in a manner that's not cocky or too aggressive. Be a gentleman. Show her that chivalry does still exist. While some girls will call guys, ask them out and be the initiator, most girls are going to wait for you to make the next move and take charge.

Also, (and this should be understood without saying), there's nothing wrong with doing "third date stuff" during a second date, or really at any time. Every situation is unique. There are certain universal qualities that all human beings share, but I view people as individuals. It's not always predictable how two people will react to one another throughout their dating experience.

* * *

What you want to avoid is being put in situations

where she's completely in control and you're waiting on her to call, in a state of limbo. In your mind, you might be thinking, "Well, if she's interested, she'll call. If not, then I'll know how she feels about me." However, this is the wrong way to go about things. What will probably happen is that you'll end up feeling like an idiot. A day will pass, followed by another, and then another, yet she still hasn't reached out. If she doesn't call you after three days, you will unquestionably give up and give in by calling her. It doesn't matter at what point you decide to call her, part of you is going to be thinking that she's thinking, "Why is he not getting the hint that I'm not interested in him?"

Ideally, you'll want to step up to the plate and be in touch with a girl at some point within the next three days (if not much sooner) after a second date. Most girls want a guy to show initiative and interest to make the next move by calling. In our modern society, it's true that texting is a useful tool of communication. However, it should not be used exclusively. Even today, most girls like receiving a phone call from a guy they like. A phone call means that you care enough to make the effort to have an actual conversation with her. If the last few guys she dated before you were predominantly texters, using the phone will make you stand out even more to her.

There could be some exceptions to this rule. There are some shy girls who don't like talking on the phone with someone they don't know that well. Some girls prefer texting, at least until they become more comfortable with someone. A girl might say to you, "Please text me, I'm not really a phone person." You should be aware of her rules and respect them.

For obvious reasons, it's almost always a good

sign if she makes the next move following the date, and calls you, although she probably won't. Her calling you could be a potential red flag, though. You want to always be on the lookout for someone who's clingy. Most girls don't want guys to act that way toward them, so why would you want to deal with somebody who might be a little too obsessive?

Not to sound harsh (it can go both ways), but most girls are needy, at least to some degree. Guys, I'm simply warning you that there are girls out there who could really make your life way more difficult than it needs to be. There are some girls who fit the mold of being overbearing, but at the same time these same girls can be extremely attractive. Herein lies the challenge we all face as guys -- often we tend to overlook potentially irreversible flaws in a girl because we find her to be attractive. We all know that God didn't put enough blood in the male body to operate more than one "head" at a time. We're only human. And guys, I understand that sometimes the one above your shoulders isn't always able to get enough blood to it.

Many guys will call the next day (after a first or second date). As previously mentioned, I prefer sending a short, simple, sweet text message to a girl following our date, either later that night after the date or the next day. If you want to call her, that's fine, but remember that there's nothing wrong with waiting at least another day before doing so. Sleep on it, and take some time for the both of you to reflect. It never hurts to let things settle a bit in your mind. Then, you can and call her. Taking a day off before calling also provides her with some space, and keeps her in her comfort zone. You'll also ensure that she won't think that you're coming on too strong or seeming too eager. Most likely, what a girl will be doing at this time is huddling up with her girlfriends and having a conference about you. You know that there's going to be some sort of list created detailing your pros and cons.

Moving forward, if she does call you, and it isn't to end things, this is likely a positive sign. All that really matters is that you're on the phone with the girl and she's still interested in you. As we've discussed in similar scenarios already, it's kind of assumed that the girl will be waiting for you to call. It's your role as the man to make the effort to reach out to her. A potential romance is called "the chase" for a reason. Most women like to be pursued, and most guys are more than happy to pursue them.

In any event, when you find yourself on the phone with her, you don't want to jump right into trying to make plans to see her again. Have a real conversation. Ask her how her day was. Relax and be confident. Hopefully there will be some rhythm and flow to your conversation. I can't reiterate enough the importance of listening to what she says, and avoid coming across like you're just forcing plans on her. Especially in the early stages, try not to whine about work (I'll expand on this more in the chapter on relationships). Keep a positive attitude on the phone, because she'll be reacting to the vibe that you put out there. Bring up a funny or notable moment that you shared on a previous date. Talk about things that you have in common, but without harping too much on the same subjects.

You'll want to ease into bringing up the next time you two will get together. Find a good transition into making plans. She expects you to bring up the subject sooner or later. I suggest that after you've shared a good conversation for a while, this is a good time to segue into seeing her again by attempting to make concrete plans for your third date. It's unlikely, but she might even be the one to ask you when she can see you again!

* * *

So here you are, once again driving over to pick her up for date number three. Continue to treat her as you have been -- pay attention to all the little things like the doors, the compliments, and, of course, picking up the check. Be observant during your time together. Notice if she's cold or not, and if so, be kind and offer her your jacket.

Depending on where the two of you are physically, you might want to hold her close. As we've previously discussed, you can either hold hands or do the her-hand-on-your-arm move. If the two of you are going to be hanging out in one particular area for a while, make sure that she's comfortable there. Be aware of the elements and overall atmosphere around you. Remember, girls can be delicate and seem to get cold or hot more easily than you do!

It doesn't hurt to get her flowers, even if you've gotten her flowers before, but get a different kind this time. A high percentage of females love chocolate, so feel free to get some for her -- nice chocolates, not a candy bar from the register unless you know that something like Snickers is her favorite. Otherwise, get her the kind of chocolates that you find in the candy aisle, not at the register. That being said, nobody ever turns down a Reese's Peanut Butter Cup!

As far as getting her other gifts besides flowers

and chocolate, try thinking outside of the box without going overboard by spending too much money. Purchasing a teddy bear might be too much too soon for some people, but if you are confident that the girl you're seeing will think it's cute, then by all means go for it. For some girls, though, it might come across as too "relationshippy". Use your best judgment and remember that it's the thought that counts. You can even go the extra mile by placing her favorite candy in the arms of the teddy bear!

If you somehow breezed by the aforementioned teddy bear, no, you did not misread what I wrote. Seemingly silly gifts like teddy bears can have a positive impact in terms of the type of guy she'll perceive you to be. Girls like soft things. Teddy bears are soft. Girls like cute. Who would ever dispute the cuteness of a teddy bear? Just remember to remove the price tag before handing her any gift. If you're on a date at an amusement park, go ahead and try to win her that five-foot-tall stuffed animal. Just remember that you will have to lug this third wheel around for the rest of the date.

Continue to hold her hand (or do the arm-in-arm thing), wherever you are. It doesn't matter whether you're at the movies, driving somewhere, or even at home with her just hanging out on the couch. (An ideal third date, or any date to a guy, is hanging out at one of your places watching a movie). Regardless of where this date takes place, always make an effort to initiate holding hands. Be calm and cool about it, and look for an opening. You don't have to go for her hand the second you two sit on the couch. Relax, and when you finally feel comfortable and the right moment is there, go for it.

Many of you are now asking, "How do I know

when it's the right moment to make this move?" You probably want to wait around five minutes into hanging out before trying to hold hands. You don't want to wait until the last five minutes to make this move. Just about any other time is more appropriate. My advice to you is to not wait too long; go for it fairly early in the evening. By hesitating and procrastinating, you'll only build tension. The tenser you seem, the more likely she'll feel that awkwardness too. It's best to dive into it early in the evening and initiate physical contact. It's a good idea to caress the top of her hand with your free hand periodically throughout the night. Don't forget that holding hands with a girl should be done with interlocking fingers!

Establishing physical contact early let's her know that you care and that you're interested. Obviously, you don't have to hold her hand 100% of the time, just do it frequently enough to show that you're interested and happy to spend time with her. Pay attention to stuff like clammy hands or when she might have an itch, or something similar. You'll be fine, and you shouldn't have a problem sensing when it's time for a little break from holding hands.

Hopefully she'll be responsive and greet you warmly with her touch. The way she responds can be another indicator of her intentions for the evening, or even of her feelings toward you. If she is a loose-grip hand-holder, don't rule this girl out yet. Even if she's only lightly holding your hand, don't be put off right away or judge, yet. Girls like to be gentle. Take the time to look at her nails and compliment her on them. If she took the time to get them done, possibly to look prettier for you, she'll appreciate your kind words that much more. After a warm compliment is usually a good time to hold her hand.

At some point while holding her hand, you may notice that some of her nail polish has chipped or worn off. Rather than making a compliment about her nails, you're much better off going for something like "Wow, you have such soft hands." Most girls love to hear that they have soft, beautiful skin. Be sweet. I know that I've hammered this point home many times, but continue to compliment her without overdoing it. Spread out your compliments.

Here's another nice thing that you can say anytime you two are together: "I love that smell, what is that?" Get to know what she likes. Perfumes are a personal choice, and she wants you to love that scent just as much as she does. Talking about these specific interests of hers will help open her up to you that much more.

The following is also important to remember, especially when you're pursuing a new romance: if you expect to have any shot at getting laid, you should adhere to these common sense approaches. For one, it's critical that you be attentive to her throughout the night. As at dinner, at home you don't want to be fiddling with your iPhone, Blackberry, or any other electronic devices. You don't want to continually get up unnecessarily throughout the night. Do not keep checking your phone or computer for sports scores or Facebook news when there's a lovely lady sitting on your couch. Even seemingly harmless activities such as minor cleaning or organizing your place will take you away from her. She might feel like she's not a priority at the moment, and she should be! You should have taken care of all the home maintenance stuff earlier!

Most likely what you'll be doing on your third date, if not sooner, is watching a movie with her at one of your places (I suggest biting the bullet and watching a romantic comedy with her. It can only help you in the long run). After a few dates, this is what most couples do. If you're reading this book and seeking help with women, you should probably pay attention to the movie. Then, when it ends, you'll have something to talk about with her. As a guy, you might not care about the movie. All you're thinking about is the right time to go in for that kiss…or more.

If you make it through the entire movie without making out, this is not a problem. After the movie ends and a little post-movie banter, it is an opportune time for you to make your move. Look into her eyes and tell her how beautiful she looks. Listen closely to what she says next. If she says, "Aww, thank you. You look pretty good yourself," it sounds like she's giving you an opening for a kiss.

Depending on how far you've gotten physically, you may not need to ask for a kiss. If this is going to be your first kiss, as I previously mentioned, you have the option to ask for it. Have confidence and be straightforward. Move in a little closer to her, and in a normal, relaxed tone ask, "Would you mind if I gave you a kiss?" If she leans in, you're in. Go for the kiss. What I like to do is two quick kisses first, and then proceed slowly with the tongue. Two pecks and a slow tongue is a good start for any make-out session, and especially for a first one.

Put your arms around her and gradually kiss her with increasing fervor. Slowly make the physical interaction more passionate by caressing her cheeks with your hands and by running your fingers slowly through her hair. Feel out the situation and gauge how aggressive she's being in caressing you back. If she moans, it's likely a sign to go forward to the next phase, which I like to refer to as "titty time!"

Just so we're on the same page, I define second base (or hitting a double) as titty time. Third base is hand-jobs, fingering, or oral sex; a home run is obviously sexual intercourse.

If she doesn't grab your wrist as you attempt to put your hand either on or up her shirt, proceed. Reach with one hand and snap off her bra. This may sound challenging, but follow the next few sentences closely:

When you have time, go into a store that sells bras where you are unlikely to run into anybody you know, a place that employs people you will hopefully never see again. Or if you can, borrow a bra from a friend or family member and practice removing a bra using a pillow. If you practice, the odds of you removing your girl's bra using one hand on the first try increases dramatically.

I've given you a specific sequence so far, but pinpointing how to "fool around" for everyone is difficult. People share unique chemistries and idiosyncrasies. As the old adage goes, "Just do what feels natural." There's no textbook way to go about getting to first base and beyond.

As guys, it's normal to have a "get what you can" mentality, but we must also understand that the girl has the final say of if and when you two have sexual intercourse. If she says to stop at any point, you must obey immediately. It doesn't matter if you're in the beginning of intercourse, in the middle, or near the end, you must pull out the second she says stop. Remember, this rule applies to any sexual acts, not just intercourse.

If you have to ask, "At what point is it okay for my clothes to start to come off?", the answer is when her clothes start to come off, either by her taking them off on her own or by you helping the process along. It is okay for you to go ahead and take your own shoes and socks off, presuming your feet don't smell. If you're at home and you have sweaty feet, it's not a bad idea to change your socks. Do it discreetly, so she doesn't see what you're doing. It's always polite, and less embarrassing (for you) to take care of any hygiene-related issues privately, whether it's changing socks, putting on deodorant, or anything else along these lines.

If you think that you're about to get lucky, but she stops you from taking off her underwear and says, "I don't have sex on the first night together" (or second, or third, or whatever she says), even if you respond with something like, "But this is our third date," this will not help your cause. She will likely be turned off by your desperation, or simply by the fact that you're coming across as someone who is only looking for sex. Most girls appreciate a guy who shows patience and is willing to put in the time. Assuming that it's not a one-night stand and you've gone out on a few dates, she wants to see that getting to know her is your highest priority -- and that's getting to know who she is as person, and not just how she is in bed!

So, at any point in the midst of fooling around, if she says to slow down or stop, I can't repeat enough the importance of respecting her demands. Even if you feel like you've put the time, the money, the dates, the effort, and said and done all the right things to this point, she's still in no way, shape, or form obligated to do anything with you. Even though it may be your third date, it doesn't matter. Guys, this is not the end of the world. You have to respect her territory. It's all about her.

There's no reason to feel rejected. Don't feel hurt if she doesn't go as far with you as you wanted. Do not sigh or mumble "whatever" when she asks you to slow down. Do not beg or whine, or say or do anything that makes it seem like the only thing on your mind is sex. You want to show her that you have the confidence you will eventually "get her." Play it cool. There's no reason why you shouldn't continue to enjoy each other's company. Who knows, perhaps hitting a double or a triple that night isn't out of the question just yet.

Girls tend to make guys earn the privilege of having sexual intercourse with them. There are many reasons why a girl might not seem super-eager to have sex with you. Many of these reasons will have nothing to do with you. Regardless of how things are developing between you guys, she's still going to have her own set of rules.

Let me tell you a story that highlights the importance of showing patience with a girl. Some time ago, I went on a date with a girl named Julia. I could tell from the outset that she was very attracted to me. We had gone out on a few dates, and one night we were out again together. We were both feeling pretty good and a little tipsy. At some point she whispered in my ear, "Is it time to go back to your place?" Needless to say, minutes later we were back at my apartment. Seconds after walking through the door, she was aggressively tearing my clothes off. Things were getting hot and heavy, and we started to have sex.

Seconds after we began having sex, out of

nowhere she grabs me, pushes me off of her, and says, "We can't have sex tonight!" I asked her if everything was okay or whether I hurt her, or if it was something I said or did. She responded by telling me, "No. Everything was perfect. I just don't want our first time to be this way."

In my mind, this wasn't a satisfying explanation. What could she have meant by, "I just don't want our first time to be this way."? I'll acknowledge that neither one of us was completely sober at the time, but this was far from a one-night stand. At the end of the day, I did care about her and was genuinely interested in seeing where our romance was going.

Sure, I was disappointed that we abruptly stopped, but I wasn't about to press her on the subject. I played it cool and put my boxers back on to make her feel more at ease. She thanked me for being such a gentleman and for being so understanding. For the rest of the night, we cuddled, enjoyed each other's company, and fell asleep peacefully together.

You guys can say what you want about how this night went down and the actions I took, but a week later she came back to my place -- this time wearing four-inch silver stiletto heels and a black trench coat. I'll let you imagine what was underneath that coat. It goes without saying that we picked up where we left off the previous week and had a great time together. So, don't ever underestimate the value of showing patience with a girl, and showing her the respect she deserves!

* * *

While we're on the subject of sex, I would like talk

about sexually transmitted diseases for a moment. STD's are a real and serious problem, especially in today's society. It's not uncommon for a girl to want you to get tested before she decides that she's going to let you become sexually active with her. If you really like this girl, be considerate and do this for her.

For example, one time a girlfriend of mine forced me to get tested. I'm not saying that she held a gun to my head, but until I did what was asked, I wouldn't be "getting any" from her. I agreed to get tested, under the condition that she would too. I wasn't trying to turn this into a game, or a tit-for-tat, but it's important that both partners be on the same page, that there are no secrets when it comes to health. Guys, this is your life, and you don't want to make a bad decision that you will regret. This goes for girls too. It's completely disgraceful if somebody knowingly has an STD, but doesn't inform a new sexual partner. To me, this is one of the most vile acts a human being can commit.

I can't stress enough to you how crucial it is that partners be honest with one another about their bodies. Nobody is proud to have an STD, but more people have one than you think. An estimated 20+ million Americans contract an STD every year. There's a reason that there are medications available and commercials on television for them. Perhaps during the time our parents grew up, venereal diseases were less common, and less talked about. People were much more secretive about such issues, even with those close to them. The medical advances and technology that we have today didn't exist. There were no Google searches or WebMD's where people could research on their own before consulting with a physician. However, society has since evolved, and you should too. Be open and honest with yourself, and your sexual partner!

Back to my story: at the time we were dating, my girlfriend and I were tested at a clinic together. Afterward, I felt that much closer to her, and there was definitely more of a mutual respect, especially since both our test results came back immaculate. Because there was nothing to worry about, the trust we now shared ended up making our first sexual experience together not just good, but amazing, an experience that I will not soon forget!

If you have contracted an STD, I feel for you, and getting down on yourself is understandable. However, as cliché as this might sound, human beings aren't perfect, but we seem to find a way to get through trials and tribulations. We should always try to find a way to be thankful for what we have, and strive to live life to the fullest, because we're not going to be around forever.

There's no reason to continue to beat yourself up. I can't speak from personal experience, but I'm sure that it must sound horrible at first when you find out that you have an STD. This is an illness that you'd prefer to have not experienced, especially because it often attacks your genitalia.

I want you to understand that if you are a carrier, you are not an outcast in society. You're not alone. Don't let this one flaw determine how you view yourself and how you want others to view your character. If you are clean, cherish that. Be careful out there. Yes, things do happen to people who don't feel that they deserve such consequences, but part of living life on this planet is dealing with misfortune.

Remember that even with an ailment like herpes, severity varies from case to case. For example, I have a friend (seriously, it's not me) who has to deal with a mild case of herpes that causes outbreaks around his lips about twice a year and lasts for a two-week period. He's only contagious for a period of roughly five to seven days.

This isn't the end of the world for him, but he makes an effort to be as sanitary as possible. I have a lot of respect for him by the way he carries himself and how he takes care of this unfortunate medical condition. He's washes his hands frequently and always makes sure that nobody else drinks from his glass. He's both mature and responsible enough to be open about all this when the appropriate time comes with a new girl. Depending on what ailment a person has, this determines when one should break the news to a potential sexual partner. It's not unreasonable to be open on a first date, even if your chances of scaring her away increase tenfold. It's also not unreasonable to break the news a little bit later on when you're dating someone – as long as you don't wait too long. It depends on the illness. Regardless, you must inform your partner about any relevant health issues before engaging in any type of sexual activity together.

To review, whether it's herpes or any other STD, the severity and symptoms can vary widely. I'm not going to pretend to be a medical expert, but your doctor is. If you have any fears that you may have caught something, get expert medical attention.

* * *

Back to dating: remember that if things don't seem to be going well with a girl (either physically or emotionally), and you are unhappy with anything going on (or not going on), perhaps you should consider that this girl isn't worth your time or effort. It doesn't make you a bad person to have these feelings. The point is that if the (physical) chemistry for whatever reason just isn't there, you shouldn't feel guilty about wanting to move on.

If you find out that the third date wasn't quite what you wanted or expected, reassess the evening. Did the physical element not go smoothly? Did you guys not hit it off as well as in previous dates?

Don't force the issue with a situation that clearly isn't going well. Guys, you must remember that you will meet plenty of women in your life, and there is no reason to put all of your eggs in one basket. Don't be afraid to start a new relationship. It's healthy to take that leap of faith and jump off the cliff, and build your wings on the way down. On the other extreme, don't be alarmed if it seems like your relationship is moving fast. Sometimes it's the right move become serious after only a short period of time. People actually do sometimes find themselves on the exact same page as one another! I refer to this as the early stages of falling in love.

It's best to not make any assumptions about how serious a relationship will go with a girl. It's absurd to think that every first date is going to be with the girl you are going to marry. Most guys realize this, but for those of you out there who don't, be careful with these types of thoughts. It's good to have standards. Be reasonable and don't expect to find a wife right away. Go into it looking for some things in common with a girl that you're interested in. Often overlooked, it is the simple connections that are the building blocks of strong, lasting relationships.

If the third date does eventually turn into a new

relationship, good for you. On the flipside, if the third date doesn't work out, don't get down on yourself. Either way, get out there and date, break hearts, get yours broken, and have some valuable experiences. Don't be afraid to make mistakes. Trust me, you'll laugh looking back as an older and wiser person, and as someone who's glad to have read this book. I want readers just like you to pick and choose what works best for you from everything we've discussed. This book isn't meant to be your only bible. It's just one guy sharing his honest feelings, and philosophies. No matter how bleak the dating world can seem at times, always know that there's still plenty of hope and reasons that you will get together with someone new, and probably sooner than you think!

Chapter 11: Sex & Dating

So you finally had sex with her and want to again. Let's say you hit that home run on your third date (if not earlier). I'm going to go out on a limb and say that you made plans to see her again. After all, we're discussing a girl who you've been pursuing for some time, and she is not a one-night stand. For those of you who are only looking for a piece of ass and finally got it from a girl who you've gone out with a few times, that's your prerogative. However, it is in poor taste to "hit it and quit it" (or "toot it and boot it"), and definitely if you've been leading a girl on by behaving as if you're interested in something more. Once again, this book isn't a "how to get laid" manual. It's more about helping you build your confidence so that you can better pursue a girl who you really like, and win her heart.

A significant part of finding happiness in a relationship is enjoying the sexual aspect -- and I'm not just talking about your enjoyment, guys, but also the importance of keeping her satisfied by returning the favor. This book isn't intended to be a guide to sex like the Kama Sutra, but I'd like to go over a few basic concepts. To many of you, this may not be new information, but don't be afraid to read this advice with an open mind. At the very least, some of what I'm about to talk about could help reaffirm preconceived notions that you have about sex.

If you know that you are going to see your girl later on that day or night, it's not a bad idea to "rub one out" beforehand. I'm sure that you want to be able to last as long as possible in bed with her. So, when you have some extra time before a date, take care of business. I prefer to never leave the house with a "loaded gun." Most guys are aware of this strategy, but I want to express my full support of it and assure you that there's no harm in rubbing one out before you have sex. You can only benefit from it. If you're benefiting, she'll be benefiting. Who knows, maybe afterward she'll brag to her friends about you! (Girls talk to each other about this type of stuff). As much as guys like to pretend that it's not always true, we not only all have big egos but fragile ones, and we would much prefer to have our sexual prowess talked about in a positive light.

We could discuss all sorts of sexual positions and techniques, but to each their own, because what turns one person on might not stimulate someone else. Preferences and boundaries are determined by each couple. That said, I want to share pointers that will apply to a very high percentage of sexual relationships.

Girls want you to be loving, but also aggressive. Remember, though, females can be fickle, so it's not always the right time to be aggressive, or even kinky. Feel out the situation and mood, and do your best to read what she wants. More than likely, she is going to let you know whether or not something you do (or want to do) is fair game. Guys, I urge you to be assertive and take charge. Believe me, if you do something that she isn't into, she'll let you know. She might even tell you what she's in the mood for, or what she likes. It never hurts to ask a girl what she likes, but you want to set the tone by taking charge. These ideas, along with the process of trial and error, will point you in the right direction -- whether that means making love gently or fucking like animals!

It's crucial that sexual partners be open with one another and able to communicate about sex.

It's not always the right moment to "throw her around," but you want to be able to open up a side that will allow her to become kinkier with you. Depending on what you're into, even taking photos and shooting home videos could be possibilities. But be careful: this could come back to haunt you later, because once something finds its way onto the Internet, there's no turning back!

There's a chance that your girl is even kinkier than you think. Once you delve into that side of a girl, you've achieved a certain level of intimacy and trust with her. There's a part of almost every girl that's a nymphomaniac buried inside, or at least that's the hope we all share as guys.

A common complaint that I hear from women is that guys aren't assertive or aggressive enough. Believe it or not, some females even confess to me that their men don't enjoy sex enough! Don't be afraid to take charge when the opportunity is there. Try to keep the sexual aspect of the relationship both spontaneous and unpredictable at times. You want to keep her guessing and on her toes -- then bust out the fury when the right moment presents itself to you. There's nothing wrong with a little hair pulling and ass-slapping as you're giving it to your girl from behind! Be a little forceful when you grab her hair or her bottom, without being too forceful, of course.

When a relationship is in its early phase, sometimes partners feel the need to impress each other with his or her sexual prowess. I'm not saying that it's frowned upon to have sex multiple times a day, but don't rush into things just because you assume that's what the other person wants. This could even turn off the other person, because s/he might feel as if the other partner is purely interested in sex, and not so much the person they're with.

* * *

What about everything besides the sex? Perhaps you're stuck in that weird in-between phase during which your relationship with this girl is undefined. "Are we dating?" "Are we in a relationship?" "Are we fuck buddies?" "Will she call me?" "Should I call her?" "How was I in bed?" More than likely she's asking the same questions. You could be asking yourself, "Should I assume that the next time we hang out that we're going to have sex?" Another all-important question she might bring up is: "What are we?" Perhaps you are asking, "What should I do now?" "Should I bring up questions about our 'status'?" I realize that this can be an awkward phase during which there are more questions than answers, but the best advice I can give you is to keep in mind that every scenario is unique.

It's crucial that you have a response to her possible question: "Where is this going?" This can be a very touchy situation depending on how you respond, particularly if she wants a relationship, but might not be confident that you want the same thing. There are a few key phrases that you can use to diffuse some of the tension in these sticky interactions. If you're genuinely unsure about what you want, tell her that you want to take things slowly and get to know her more. Even if you are unsure about a serious relationship, tell her, "I'm not interested in seeing anybody else right now." It doesn't hurt to turn it around a bit, too, and put the focus on her. Ask her where she sees herself, not only with you, but in her life in general.

You don't want to feel blindsided, so try to be ready with a response for these tough questions. If you really do like this girl, come right out and say something as blunt as, "I want to be honest with you. I really like you, and I hope that you feel the same way." If you truly want to be with this girl, consider saying something like, "Not to rush you or anything, but I was wondering if we could start seeing each other exclusively." You could also go with, "Listen, I don't know how you feel, but I feel like we're progressing forward, and I would really like to be exclusive with you."

Be honest with her, but don't go overboard. It might not be such a great idea to tell this girl that you love her just yet -- there will be more on the "L word" in the next chapter. Anyway, be sure to give her a chance to respond. Depending on how she responds, you can either push the subject a little further or back away if she's clearly not ready or desiring to take your romance to the next level yet.

Some girls will wait for you to bring up the often-dreaded subject of "What are we?" The rule of thumb for me is to try not to lead girls on. Manipulation is a part of human nature, but some people are only occasionally guilty of it, while others make it a habit. There's only so far you can get with this type of behavior before bad feelings arise, quickly followed by unnecessary drama.

Ask yourself if you want to be single, or if you are truly ready for a relationship. If she's not worth giving up your single life for, that's your choice. Part of having a girlfriend is being prepared to lose time spent with your video games and your boys. Poker night might not happen as often. You're going have to learn to compromise and realize that you might not be able to watch football for 12 hours straight on Sundays. Also, you'll now have to remember to always put the toilet seat back down after peeing!

Giving up all this might seem like a frightening scenario to many guys, but we all know women are worth making huge, life-altering sacrifices for. We can only hope that we will someday find someone who is willing to make at least a few sacrifices for us. We'll talk about these matters soon enough when we examine the dynamics of relationships.

So your single life as you know it could be over. As you're reading this, you might be thinking: "But Lance, I've only been out with this girl a few times. Why are we considering a serious relationship so fast?" It's not that you're necessarily looking to get into something serious fast, but whether you like it or not, it can happen sooner than you think. It depends on what the two of you are looking for at this point in your lives. If you want an exclusive relationship and you're ready for one, and if the chemistry is there with this girl, why not go for it?

Depending on age, maturity, and other factors, most girls are looking for a relationship. They might say that they aren't looking to get "involved" right now, but that's just because the right guy hasn't come along yet. Ask yourself if you want to be that guy. There's no right or wrong answer, but this is your life. Put a little extra thought into how you feel when deciding what you want. Don't be afraid to consider your own feelings. Whether we want to admit it or not, we all have them in there somewhere, so why not let your feelings carry significant weight when it comes to important decisions? Sometimes it's actually best to not overanalyze by reviewing a list of pros and cons about the person you're dating. You know what I'm talking about -- those lists you create with your girlfriends or buddies. Oh, just take the leap already, follow your heart, and go for it!

But be careful when you hear from her, "I just want to take it slow." She could really want to take things slowly, and probably does, but don't rule out that she could be letting you down gradually without you knowing it. When a girl likes you, she will show it, and you will know it! She will text, call, email, Facebook, etc. She will contact you, and she will make time to see you. If she isn't into you, you will see one-line text responses and your phone calls will either be short or go unreturned. Above all else, she'll always seem to be too busy to hang out.

When a girl says she wants to take it slowly, you must respect her wishes. These are the rules that she has set forth. Every girl is going to have her own ways to conduct business, some of which you might think are illogical, but it does not matter. To some degree, one might say that she has you by the balls. If you want to be less graphic but stick with a ball reference, let's say the ball is entirely in her court. You can't force the issue much further by broaching the subject, so you're more or less playing the waiting game at this point. You must figure out ways to show her that you want to be with her, but without being too overwhelming.

It's not fun feeling like you're in limbo, but you must try your best to stay positive about the situation. Even if you're not officially a couple yet, ask yourself, "Am I still having a good time and continuing to connect with this girl?" If the answer is yes to both questions, pursuing things further is probably worthwhile.

Live your life to its fullest, even if at the moment you're in limbo. Embrace the time that you're spending with her, even if you're not sure exactly where you two are going. You're still in the early stages of getting to know her, and whether or not this is the person you'll be spending the rest of your life with, who knows? Be cool, don't force it, and let things happen naturally. Despite the times when things don't work out in your favor, I can't emphasize enough the importance of trying. It's an old lesson, and we've already mentioned how terrible regret is, but let me remind you one more time that it's better to have tried, than to not have tried at all!

If a girl isn't sure about you but you haven't been outright rejected, take her out again, or even a couple of more times. Show her more about you, and learn more about her. Open yourself up and show her what makes you, you. Share your interests with her. If you like baseball, take her to a game. If she's an avid reader and drinks coffee, take her to a coffee shop or a bookstore. If she likes rides, take her to an amusement park. You understand what I'm getting at here.

You don't ever want to force a relationship on a girl. This is the antithesis of keeping her in that all-important comfort zone. Females do not find ultimatums attractive. You have to be patient, and remember that you're not always in charge. Once again, she's going to abide by her own regulations. Being overly persistent by repeatedly telling a girl that you want to be with her might make her uncomfortable, and make you come off as needy, or even a bit controlling. This is especially true in cases in which you've only recently met a girl. I'm not trying to discourage you from being honest with the girls you're dating, but there's no urgency to declare that you want a relationship ASAP.

Before you dive into a relationship, concentrate on having fun, and figure out when you will see her next. Think about what specific plans you can make to spend more time with her. It's never a bad idea to invite her over to your place and make dinner for two. If the only things you know how to make are microwaveable, feel free to pick up food, or order in something that's higher quality than what you might eat for dinner on an average night alone. Recall some likes and dislikes of her palette when considering food choices. She'll appreciate your efforts, whether you cook her an amazing meal or you just order in a dinner that you know she'll love. She might invite you over to her place, or she might rather go out to dinner. Be flexible and open-minded when it comes to last-minute changes. It's good to show a girl that you can be spontaneous and able to roll with the punches.

Furthermore, you can try to play it cool and see where things go. You don't have to bring up status. Neither party really has to, but if you feel the need to broach the topic, it's not wrong to do so. In fact, she might be waiting for you to do just that. Don't be afraid of coming on too strong if you truly want to be exclusive. I've talked about being the first person to say goodbye during phone conversations, and a similar philosophy applies here: it can be a positive to beat her to the punch and bring up your desire to be in an exclusive relationship. By now, there's a good chance that the two of you won't be clueless about where you two stand. You've gotten a sense of each other's personalities, where you are in life, and hopefully what you are looking for in a relationship.

Every situation is different, but be smart. Realize that people in their 20's, especially their early 20's, are less likely to be ready for a real commitment. Age is not the only factor in determining preparedness for a relationship, but maturity levels often coincide with age. Sure, a 19-year-old or a 20-year-old can have a happy, successful long term relationship, but I think that most people this young don't really know who they are yet, so how can they make such grown-up decisions about their lives and futures? Of course, there are exceptions, and once in a while I'll meet someone in his or her early 20's who is mature way beyond their years. Often, uncontrollable circumstances can force people to grow up in a hurry.

To give a quick example, I met this girl Suzi on Halloween night several years ago. I ended up having an incredible heart-to-heart conversation with her. Dressed up as a Spartan warrior in a crowded bar, having a serious discussion about life is not something I had anticipated that night. Surprisingly, she began to open up to me and told me how her father often left the family for long periods of time, starting when Suzi was a little girl. She was the oldest of three kids, and after her father had left for good, money became really tight.

Suzi had no choice but to help take care of her younger siblings while her mom worked two jobs. Suzi cooked, cleaned, did laundry, and helped out with homework. At the age of 12, she was forced to do everything that a parent should do. When people are put in situations like this, often they have no choice but to grow up fast and mature at a much earlier age. I particularly admired how she had no regrets, and how she never felt sorry for herself for never having a normal childhood. Suzi didn't hold a grudge about the difficult hand that life had dealt her. She was actually quite proud of the person she had became, and after talking to her, I was too.

* * *

So guys, don't be afraid to get out there. Meet plenty of women, and make mistakes, just try not to get any diseases or impregnate anyone! That's not what I mean by "make mistakes." What I mean is going out with girls who might not be your "type," women with whom you might not be 100% compatible. In return you'll learn more about yourself and what makes you happy (and not so happy too). Get out there and go on dates with many women. If you're not exclusive with anyone, it's more than acceptable to continue meeting new people. Whatever your outlook is before you're ready to settle down, you're likely to learn a lot about dating, and your perspective will evolve over time.

On the opposite end of the age spectrum, not all 30-somethings, or even 40-somethings, are ready to commit to a long-term serious relationship. The key is to be honest with yourself and not get involved in something that you will regret. It's one thing for either a guy or a girl to be honest and express a desire for a relationship, but nobody wants to be forced into one and given ultimatums. Nobody should force another person into a situation that s/he isn't ready for or doesn't want. That's not love! I'm not going to define "love" for you, because love is something unique to every individual.

The only elements that matter are that the two of you about to enter a relationship share common bonds, mutual feelings, and of course, a sexual attraction to each another.

Even if you're not "on the prowl" trying to meet someone, life is unpredictable, and who knows what the future holds in store. We don't control everything that happens to us, but we do have some say in how our futures can be shaped. So, make your decisions wisely and enjoy the ride. Humor me, and assume we only live once. We should embrace life to its fullest by having a good time, but also by gaining wisdom through our successes and missteps along the way. Perhaps you'll meet someone who you fall in love with at first sight. Perhaps an ex will come back into your life and you'll decide that you want to rekindle that old flame. You will deal with these opportunities as they come. There's no possible way to even attempt to prepare for something that you cannot predict.

People say that chivalry is dead, and maybe it is to a certain degree. In my viewpoint, though, I encourage guys to aspire toward a certain level of nobility that is reflected in the way they treat women. I see nothing wrong with focusing on one girl at a time, particularly one who's showing a considerable amount of interest in you, and with whom you've been on several dates. In fact, I encourage this. If the attraction and feelings are there, then don't be afraid to take things to the next level.

Chapter 12: Timing

Before jumping into relationships, I wanted to take a moment to talk about something very important -- timing. This is something that will likely affect you at one point or another in your life. It's important to understand how timing can be problematic when starting a relationship. Where a person is in his/her life at any given time can greatly affect whether or not s/he is capable of being in a committed relationship. A job or financial stability could come into play. More significantly, someone's emotional state will greatly affect his or her decision-making, and this will in turn affect you too. If a person recently went through a traumatic experience, s/he might not be ready to commit to you. If someone went through a difficult break-up after a long-term relationship, she might not be ready to start a new one so soon. Getting into a new relationship takes effort and patience, but also luck, because timing can be a bitch.

Let me illustrate this further by sharing a couple of stories, where past events had a strong influence on feelings that led to decisions in the present. Not too long ago, I went on a weekend getaway with a female friend of mine named Romi. She was a Pilates instructor who I met at our rock climbing gym. We hung out a couple of times outside of the gym on a purely platonic level. She was an energetic, drama-free girl, and an absolute blast to be around.

Originally, I was supposed to take a trip to Palm Springs with my girlfriend at the time. However, three weeks prior, we broke up. Unable to receive a refund, I began to think about who I could take as a substitute to join me for this resort and spa getaway. Almost immediately, Romi came to mind, and fortunately, she also happened to be available. I made sure that she understood that this wasn't a romantic gesture on my part and that we would only be going as friends. I texted her this, "Not trying to make a move on you, lol…just thought you'd be a fun person to chill with, who'd like to have fun in the sun..." After I sent her this spiel, she happily agreed to join me, probably because she didn't feel uncomfortable with my invitation. Guys, it all comes back to keeping the girl in that all-important comfort zone.

Anyway, the second we arrived at our destination, it was a non-stop good time. We swam, ate, drank, and partied. Then, after a few drinks, we slow danced together. A song ended and we found ourselves holding one another, eyes locked. Then, without thinking, I blurted out, "What's going on here?" She replied, "What do you mean?" I then said, "Well, we really seem to be connecting. I can't tell you how thrilled I am knowing that we still have two full days left here." She responded with, "Me too, I really think that this is going to be an incredible weekend." Moments later, she asked me, "So, how long have you been single?" I probably took a little too much time before responding, but I eventually confessed that I had just broken up with a girl whom I had been dating for a little more than a year. Not wanting her to think that she was a rebound girl, I told her, "I don't want you to think I invited you here for the wrong reasons." For those of you who don't know, a "rebound girl" is the first new girl you sleep with after a recent breakup. This is someone a person typically only has sex with, without the potential for a relationship.

On that weekend, I really needed to get away with a friend who was cool, chill, and had no hang-ups, someone drama-free who I could just be myself around. As I was telling her all of these things, I noticed that she started to smile and even laugh. I asked her what she was smiling about, and that's when she confessed that she had just recently gotten out of a relationship as well! Her relationship was with a guy she'd been with for almost five years! I then said, "Let's call a spade a spade. We're both in two crazy, mixed-up states of mind right now because of what's gone on in our lives. We're trying to ground ourselves…pick up pieces, and move on." We both were relieved. I went on, "We know we're both great people and attractive people. I think we both know that the timing just isn't right." I was thrilled when she replied, "I can't believe it. You're saying the exact things that are on my mind right now." I told her, "I still want to hang out, and who knows, down the road we might end up together."

We hugged and thanked one another for being so understanding. Then we did some shots, followed by cannonballs into the pool. We had an extremely fun weekend together. Despite a part of me wishing that this vacation had happened with my ex, or that it had ended up being a romantic one with Romi, I was actually happy to find comfort in a friend who was in a similar situation. This brings up another important lesson: it's crucial to get a sense of where a potential love interest is coming from; otherwise one might act hastily and jump to conclusions.

Now, I know what many of you guys (and even

girls) out there are thinking. You think that I'm lame for passing up a possible opportunity to hook up. Believe me, guys, it wasn't easy to pass on a chance of a night of romance, especially with such an attractive girl. Honestly, though, I look back on that weekend with no regrets, and I feel proud that I was able to exhibit maturity by showing restraint. If you're looking to be a player, by getting laid as much as possible, that's fine. But for those of you who are looking for something more, you don't have to jump at every chance to get laid. You don't have to have the mentality of, "Well, I don't know when the next time that an opportunity like this will come to me, so I better take advantage of it." Guys, you should have some self-respect and confidence, knowing that you will get laid soon enough, when the moment is right for both parties.

Now let's think about the potential consequences should Romi or I have been in a situation where a move went unreciprocated. Remember that this conversation happened on the very first night of the weekend. We could've gone from having an incredible weekend together to a weekend of uncomfortable awkwardness, trapped together far away from home. Someone's feelings could've been hurt. If we were both coming from different situations, in different states of mind, perhaps the weekend could've turned out another way. Unfortunately in life, for good or bad, timing is everything.

* * *

More recently, I was crushing on a girl named Tara, who I had run into several times at the rock climbing gym as well (maybe it's the gym's fault). Anyway, I had only seen her a handful of times, but I always noticed her smile (and body, too, of course). I was intrigued and wanted to get to know her. Eventually, I built up the courage to go up and talk to her, after only a few waves and nods hello in passing. After a few more times of running into her at the gym and sharing short conversations, nice goodbye hugs became the norm. Things seemed to be going well, so I felt it would be appropriate to ask for her phone number, which she gladly gave to me. I invited her to go on an outdoor rock climb. She thought it was a great idea and told me that she happened to be free that weekend. Boom. Plans were made for us to go climbing with a group of people. I had no problem with this being a group outing. I just wanted to get a chance to spend more time with her.

We seemed to click from the start, and everybody had a great time that weekend. Even though it was a group outing, we paired up and climbed most of the routes together, while the other pairs climbed nearby. We ended up climbing really well together, pushing each other to get to the top of the mountain. It went so well that more plans were made to climb at the gym and elsewhere, as climbing buddies.

After several more meet-ups at the gym, we started hanging out together afterward, and having dinner together. Soon after the dinners, we found ourselves hanging out at her place watching movies, chatting, and having a nice time together. Things clicked for us, and the first kiss happened one night after a great conversation -- when we were both still in our sweaty, smelly climbing gear! We were so much in the moment that this didn't even matter to us.

Valentine's Day was a couple of weeks away at the time, and I remember the subject came up one night when we were climbing together at the gym. She mentioned that the previous year, she spent Valentine's Day alone at the gym. Upon hearing that she was alone for Valentine's Day last year, and not wanting to be alone myself that year, I made the bold move of asking her out. She seemed very excited and maybe a bit nervous too, since I had put her on spot. What choice did I have? I had this beautiful girl right in front of me, we had been hanging out, and even shared our first kiss. This seemed like a natural progression to me.

So, it was finally Valentine's Day, and because she worked close to my workplace, I decided to surprise her with a personal delivery of flowers at lunchtime. She was shocked to see me and was grinning ear to ear, very appreciative of my gesture. She proudly introduced me to some of her coworkers. That night I picked her up, and we went to a nice restaurant on the ocean in Malibu. We had an extremely fun, romantic dinner, filled with laughter and great conversation.

In the weeks after, we spent even more time together, but while I became more attached to her, I started to feel like she was slowly backing away. Then, all of a sudden, she went cold turkey. She stopped responding to my texts and phone calls. Two weeks of nothing. I was going nuts, wondering what went wrong, and what I had done to deserve this mistreatment. Through the grapevine, I found out that she was going on a rock climbing trip for her birthday with all of our friends, and I wasn't invited. The day before she flew out for the trip, I texted her, asking if I could drop off birthday gifts. These presents would be specifically sentimental to her, and I wanted to make sure that she received them. It would have been nice to give them to her in person, but I asked if I could at least drop them off at her work or mail them. She finally reached out and responded by saying that she could meet up after work, before she left for the trip.

When I got to her office, she confessed that she could tell that my feelings were growing a lot faster than hers, and she repeated that she was just coming out of an on-and-off five-year relationship. She told me that when she first met me, she finally started to realize that she could officially be done with her ex. But unfortunately for me, now she was saying that she needed some "me time." She said that she hadn't been single in a long time, and that she needed a breather. She said that she didn't know how to express this to me.

Looking back, there were signs that I should have picked up, that I missed. I was so infatuated with her and eager to get to know her, that I didn't consider how much of her past with her ex was affecting us. It's not like her past relationship never came up in conversation, but I suppose that I made the decision to downplay this by blocking it out. She apologized for her actions and said she wanted to just be friends. She told me that she really wanted to be that girl for me, but she couldn't at that time. She wished that she could give me more, and really wanted to, but she needed more time before she'd be ready to commit to another relationship. I respected her for this, and I will always care for her. There's a part of me that hurts to know that a great girl slipped through my fingers, but at least I learned a lesson about how one person can be fully invested and in the moment, without realizing that the other person is in a completely different mindset. The timing was just off. Timing ultimately wrecked me and what could have been an amazing relationship for us.

I could share more stories about how crucial timing is, but in all honesty, the most important tip I can give is to pay attention to the signs, including what a girl says. Don't be blinded by your emotions and initial attraction to a girl. Although both of my stories in this chapter dealt with girls who had just gotten out of long-term relationships, there are many more examples of how bad timing can derail a potential romance. Be sure to be realistic, because as much as you want things to work out, it might not be in the cards, and in the end, it's often no one's fault. It's just bad timing.

Chapter 13: Relationships

"So, the million dollar question -- Where do you find true love? You don't. It finds you -- when and where you least expect it, and often when it's most inconvenient. And it is during that time that if it is right, then absolutely nothing else matters, all the love songs aren't so corny, and everything is in color."
-Anonymous

It's true. The wonderful memories that you'll create and share together in a loving relationship are endless. However, I can't stress enough the importance of considering one last time all of the aspects that you cherish about being a single guy -- and what you will be giving up once you make a commitment. What first comes to my mind is the freedom to see any girl you want, but more important is the overall freedom that you sacrifice upon entering a new relationship. As a single guy, you report to no one but yourself. When it comes to finances, you don't have the added expense of a girlfriend. Think about what the birthdays, anniversaries, Valentine's Days, Christmases, Chanukahs, Kwanzaas, and other special occasions will cost you. Guys, I know that this is a time in your life when you'll never have more personal freedom, but life is all about the choices we make. This is it. Are you finally ready to begin a new life in a committed relationship?

If the answer is yes, you're going to have to work at it by constantly making an effort to keep the ship sailing smoothly. Successful relationships require a lot of time, energy, and as previously mentioned, sufficient funds. A relationship requires maintenance, much like a new car, house, or computer.

You may be asking yourself, "Now that I've found someone significant who could potentially be somebody I go the distance with, how do I maintain a happy relationship with her?" While there is no exact formula, there are certain ideas that you can apply that will be helpful.

Before I give you pointers, I want to sympathize with everyone who is not at this point, because I know how hard it can be to meet someone, and how challenging it can be to open your heart to another soul. Even when both parties have honest, loving intentions, things don't always work out, and like I've said it's often not just one person's fault.

Let's move on to some specifics of what you can do to keep your girl happy. The majority of what I'm going to share isn't all about grand gestures. It's not always about spending tons of money or writing long, sappy love letters. It's the day-to-day little things that you do for her that will bring the biggest smile to her face. It is the seemingly insignificant but consistent gestures that will help bring more security and trust to your relationship.

* * *

First of all, try not to bring work home with you. What I mean by this is: say you had an awful day at work. You woke up in the morning, spilled coffee on your shirt, and then on your way to the office, you were pulled over. The officer promptly wrote you a pricey ticket, despite your plea for mercy. This hectic beginning to your day caused you to be late to work. Your boss wasn't thrilled and you fell behind on your assignments. Everyone has days like these, but all we can do is hope that they come around rarely.

I'm not telling you that you can't ever complain about work. Just try to listen to her first and give her your attention when you come home in the evening, if you live with your girlfriend. The same principle applies to phone conversations, or whenever you two meet after the workday ends. Whatever has occurred, you don't want to bombard a girl with all of your life problems the very second you talk to her. If it's a casual vent that you need to get out of your system, hopefully you're with somebody who will provide comfort and listen to you, by sensing when you're upset and feeling down in the proverbial dumps. I shouldn't have to say this, but if there's big news or an emergency, you shouldn't hesitate to be vocal right away.

Unfortunately, there is a bit of a double standard here. Your girl has more of a right to bitch about whatever it is that didn't go her way during the course of that day. This might sound unfair, but we should aspire to be more noble and understanding. We should jump at the chance to make it all about her.

If you're someone who brings work home with you on a regular basis, this only brings negative energy into the relationship. One thing that you must know is that we all feed off of each other's vibes and emotions. If you enter the room upset, even if your girl is in a good mood, soon enough you're going to bring her down too. More often than not, it is the negative person who brings down the positive person, not the other way around. In order for the person who's upset to feel better, they have to be willing and open. You have to let down your guard and allow the other person the opportunity to make you feel better.

Part of maturing in a relationship is learning to pick your battles by exercising restraint. If a girl truly loves you, you will find the right time to vent about your job, or whatever is troubling you. If you're one of the vast majority of Americans who don't like their boss, co-workers, salary, hours, or job in general, complaining about the same issues over and over again will get you nowhere fast in your relationship. There's only so much that a girl wants to hear when it comes to the same story repeated endlessly.

If you exercise a little restraint, however, your work dilemma will seem more meaningful to your girl. If you're not a frequent complainer, but occasionally feel the need to vent, your girl will know that you're genuinely unhappy.

Perhaps before you know it, one of you will crack a joke about your situation at work. In the midst of laughter, you might forget about your irritating co-worker and suddenly remember how smart, beautiful, lovable, and funny your girl is. You might think that this section is corny, but it's these little moments that help build the foundation of your relationship and future with your girl. These seemingly trivial moments define the core of your relationship.

Think about the so-called quality time you spend with your girl. The two of you should be talking about things that you like to talk about and doing things that you like to do together. If you're saying and doing things that make your girl smile and laugh, continue to do what you've been doing, and keep up the good work!

* * *

Figure out restaurants and places to go to, but give her choices along the way. Don't always say, "Where do you want to go?" Be assertive, be the man in the relationship, and show her a good time. The most important thing is for her to enjoy herself, and not be bored and uninterested in you. It sounds simple, but if she's having a good time, then you'll have a good time too. Keeping her smiling obviously minimizes your stress. It sounds basic, but if your girl is happy and your relationship isn't having major issues, then you ought to be pleased with how it's going. If she isn't happy, then soon enough (if not already) you will become unhappy too.

When you two are out together in social situations, remember that she is your lady, your pride and joy, your princess. In general, make sure that you keep her close by, and hold her hand. Extend your elbow for her to grab onto as you escort her into the restaurant, bar, club, or wherever you are headed. This especially applies to when you are walking up or down any stairs. Show her affection and keep her safe. This is another old-school gesture that she's sure to appreciate. In addition, everyone in the room should know that you are a couple and that she is your woman and you are her man. Your actions ought to communicate this to everyone in the room: your woman is off-limits.

Sometimes when I'm out, I see couples behaving oddly; they seem to ignore each other entirely. It's not as if they're arguing, it's just that they appear awkward and don't really know how to express themselves. It's either that, or they have zero chemistry and major fundamental issues in their relationship. If you think a situation like this is acceptable, that's your choice. I've always felt that we shouldn't settle for dysfunctional relationships or accept what's bound to make us unhappy.

One time I was walking down Sunset Boulevard and I spotted a 70-, or even 80-year-old couple. They were holding hands while walking together. I also noticed that he was walking closest to the curb, which is the most proper way to walk down the sidewalk with your lady.

Being the outgoing person that I am, I said hello to these strangers. They both said hello in return. Instead of moving on, I asked how long they had been together. The woman responded, "We've been married 55 years." After the initial, "Wow," I went on to ask, "What's the secret to lasting so long together? Do you have any advice for me?" Their reply? "To listen to one another... You both have to be willing to bend equally."

We politely parted, and while walking away, I immediately thought to myself, "I hope I can one day experience what it's like to love someone so much, to be able to grow old with someone." I was impressed by this couple, not only because they were still affectionate with one another, but also that they felt free enough to let their feelings be known in public.

Going back to your relationship, others in the room should know that you and your girl are together. In addition to holding hands, be affectionate in other ways. This doesn't mean that you should be all over her playing tonsil hockey, but put your arm around her waist as you guys are waiting in line. Kiss her frequently, on the hand, cheek, neck, or lips. Mix it up. The point is you want to show her affection. You want other people to know that this is your woman. You want to enter the room with pride and confidence. Everyone should see you and your girl as a devoted couple, and respect it.

Avoid arguing or major disputes in public. Emotions can run high, but we as men should pride ourselves in exercising self-control. If the fight can wait until home, that's ideal. Try to settle disputes privately whenever possible; try to sit tight until a more appropriate time to resolve your dispute is available. There is no good time to fight, but if there's a way to avoid making an embarrassing scene in public, act accordingly to avoid drama that could damage your relationship. Saying hurtful things to your girl in front of other people is humiliating. You want her to feel cherished. The way you treat your girl and behave around her will greatly influence how esteemed she feels in your presence.

Remember that we live in the 21st century, and the man's role has evolved over time. This is not the 1950's, in which the man comes home from work and his woman is expected to have a hot meal ready on the kitchen table. No longer is it always the case that a man comes home to a cleaned house and folded laundry. The point is that we live in a fast-paced world, and more often than not, men and women share equal weight in the workforce. Guys in today's world often cook just as much as women, if not more.

Not every guy is going to have the skills to prepare a gourmet meal at the drop of a hat, but at the same time, it won't hurt you to develop some basic cooking skills.

Trust me: no woman is ever turned off by a guy who's capable in the kitchen. She'll appreciate you more and will feel secure in knowing that she can count on you for a good meal, at least from time to time.

So go pick up a cookbook, or change the channel to the Food Network. Call your mom, or grandma (or whoever), and ask how she prepares her world famous meatloaf. Not only will you learn from this and impress your girl, your family will be happy to know that you can make a traditional dish that's been passed down through generations. If possible, it's never a bad idea to own a barbecue grill or a hibachi grill, if that's more convenient. I believe that all guys should own a grill at some point in their lives. Most of the time, foods taste better grilled. By purchasing a grill, it might give you that spark to finally improve your cooking abilities -- and this could turn out to be one more way you can score extra points with the opposite sex.

I mentioned how the role of a man in the kitchen has evolved over time, but so has the woman's, in a different way. While many men have learned how to follow recipes, you might be surprised to find out how many girls can't prepare much beyond Easy Mac!

In my opinion, the development of women's rights and feminism have played a significant part in terms of why chivalry has been considered by many lost, or even dead, in modern society. Of course, I believe in equality and equal rights, and that a girl can do anything a guy can do, but an unfortunate byproduct of the fight to obtain such equality has been a strong trend in how men no longer treat women the way they should be treated.

* * *

Say you guys are both coming home late from work and had made plans for the evening, such as dinner and a movie. Keep her posted regarding when you think you might get out of work. You probably expect the same updates from her, so establish this type of communication. Keep her in the loop. Text her something simple like, "Sorry I'm caught up at the office, should be home around 9ish." If this ends up becoming 9:30 or 10, let her know. If the two of you had made plans to eat dinner together but you're running late, be courteous and give her the option to eat without you. If you had plans to go out to dinner but it's getting late, offer to stop on the way to bring food home.

If making simple dinner plans is a struggle, this is a problem. I can't stress enough how vital it is that the communication lines remain open as much as possible. Believe me, you're going to have a lot bigger problems in your relationship than the question of, "What are we doing for dinner?" It is so minor in the grand scheme. I'm talking to both guys and girls here. Communication and compromise are essential to any happy, growing relationship.

This means that guys can do the laundry too. Do things for her without asking, or waiting for her to request them. Listen to what she says. There are always clues to what she wants or needs you to help out with. Often, girls will beat around the bush and expect us to solve riddles, instead of telling us exactly what they want us to do. At other times, yes, she will tell you exactly what she wants.

Help out with the cleaning and other chores. Put

the dirty dishes in the dishwasher. Empty it if the dishes are clean and ready to be put away. Help out with simple jobs like hanging that framed photo she loves. If she talks about putting up shelves, get involved. Go with her to the hardware store to get the shelves, brackets, screws, etc. If you're not much of a handyman, don't be afraid to ask an employee for assistance. This probably goes without saying, but the Internet is an outstanding source for instruction to do just about anything, including putting up shelves. Use Google, or even YouTube for instruction.

Ask your girl where she keeps her brooms or vacuum. Be proactive about helping her out, but don't help and automatically expect favors in return. Do not bring up something nice that you did for her the other day when you guys are having a fight. This creates a tit-for-tat situation that will escalate the fight. Also, the next time you make a nice gesture to her, she'll question your motives and wonder if you will use it as ammunition to make her feel guilty during your next quarrel. Make these sweet gestures because you genuinely care and want to help your girl. Such generous behavior will not go unnoticed, and I bet that she'll love you even more if you continue to happily go out of your way for her.

Here's an example of what I'm talking about: if you're riding in her car and she's at the wheel, and soon after hitting the road you notice that her brakes are making loud, screeching noises, or you observe that her car is dirty both inside and out. Be enthusiastic about volunteering to take care of these matters. It's kind to ask her, "This weekend, I'd like to take your car to get an oil change and have those brakes looked at. Is that okay?" She'll be thrilled that you are taking the initiative. She'll be even more ecstatic when you pull up to her place and she sees that her car is sparkling clean.

Even though we have discussed how the roles of men and women have changed over time, it is my belief that certain roles of men and women will always remain constant. Don't doubt the strength, intelligence, or independence of a girl, but keep in mind that she'll feel much more comfortable knowing that she can rely on you for the typical duties that society has given to males. Take care of the more traditional duties as the man in the relationship, such as car-related tasks, taking out the trash, moving furniture, hanging frames, and most importantly, killing bugs or any other unwanted pests in the home. You understand what I'm getting at here.

We can even go beyond this. Part of your role as a man is to keep your girl safe, and also comfortable. As I've mentioned, observe when she's feeling warm, and do whatever you can to keep her feeling cool. Notice when she's feeling cold, and figure out how to keep her warm.

For example, I was watching a movie with a girl on my couch one time and she had her knees up high, her bare feet on the couch. Her arms were wrapped around her bent legs. I reached over and tried to tickle her feet. I realized how cold her feet were, and I said, "Put them here." Basically I sat on her feet to keep them warm. That might sound a little weird, but trust me, you won't crush your girlfriend's feet by doing this. Sure, a blanket or turning up the thermostat will do the trick, but not in the same creative, spontaneous way that using your own body heat does. Assuming your buttocks won't break her toes, she'll love this intimate, instinctual gesture on your part. She'll feel more secure. She will know that she has someone who not only cares about himself, but someone who is ready to make that extra effort for his girl.

As much as we like to joke about it, when a girl is in "that time of the month," she has legitimate reasons for behaving erratically. Mood swings are natural occurrences, so it's best that we men not always take things so personally when a girl is on her period. We especially need to show sympathy, compassion, and understanding during this time frame. It sucks, but you have to accept some irrational thinking and behavior on her part. It is up to you to decide if her behavior is related to her period, or if there's something deeper going on. You must decide if something is an insignificant tiff, or if it is behavior that truly hurts you and makes you unhappy.

If you truly love your girl, it is especially important to be extra sensitive during this time each month. Guys, we should feel lucky that we don't have to go through such a painful ordeal every month. We should get down on our knees every night and thank God that we don't have to experience such anguish on a regular basis. But let it be said, our anguish comes from the girl! Oh, just kidding...

* * *

Guys, try to remember to give your girl a massage, at least every once in a while. This is something that you should do especially when your girl isn't feeling quite like herself. During the workweek is always nice, because this is typically when she feels the most stress. Even if your girl really wants a massage, she might not always request one.

If you pay close attention to her and listen closely,

you might be able to catch her mumbling something like, "I think I slept weird last night. My neck feels a little sore." A light switch should turn on in your head. Show interest in what's bothering her. Ask what specific area of her neck is hurting. If you happen to be busy cooking, cleaning, or on your way out, promise to give her a massage later.

Later that day or night, remember what she said earlier. She will be pleasantly surprised that you actually listened to her by asking how her neck is. Say, "I would like to give you a massage. Where does it hurt?" Focus on the problematic areas and listen closely to her requests. If you're not sure how to give a proper massage, do some research. Whether you're a beginner, intermediate, or advanced when it comes to massages, I've found that YouTube has plenty of videos that go over the process step by step. If you have ever injured a girl during a massage, you probably should just pay for a professional massage therapist.

The point I'm trying to make is that she shouldn't always have to ask for a massage. I realize that you aren't going to be massaging your girl every single day, but what you want to avoid is going from giving her frequent massages to giving none at all. I understand that massaging will likely slow down over time, but continue to put yourself out there and make the effort by offering. Remember, you don't have to massage your girl for hours. Even a quick five- to ten-minute massage will always be appreciated. And to the ladies out there reading this, it's always nice to reciprocate as well.

I have another suggestion that's a sweet gesture that can go a long way with girls: when you wake up in the middle of the night to pee or to get a glass of water, etc., as you're getting back into bed, it's not a bad idea to give her a quick kiss on the cheek or neck. Even if she's not awake or completely awake, in her unconscious state of mind she'll feel your gentle kiss and that much more secure, knowing that you're really her man and care enough about her to show that you love her at all hours of the day. Along with the quick peck, softly whispering "Good night" or, if you're at that stage in your relationship, "I love you" can be a nice touch.

You're in a relationship now, and part of being in one is showing consistent affection. If you don't, you should think twice about what you want and if you should continue onward. Guys, if a girl doesn't feel like she's getting the love and affection from you that she deserves, do yourself a favor and don't hurt her anymore. Do the right thing and choose the mature option: break up with her, let her go. Let her find someone else who wants to give her the love that she deserves. If you're a girl reading this, and your man isn't giving you what you need in a relationship, consider leaving him. Make sure you've given it your all first, and exhaust all resources. Talk to him, and if you think it might help, consider going to a therapist together. All I'm suggesting is that you don't throw in the towel too early. But girls, if he seems incapable of changing his ways, starting fresh is probably a wise move for you.

Here's another example of physical affection that a couple shares: cuddling. There are couples who cuddle and there are those who don't. There are couples who always cuddle, and others who only do so once in a while. I'm not trying to tell you what you should or shouldn't do, or mold you into a cuddler per se, but I for one am very much into cuddling. Not only do I enjoy cuddling on the couch, I also love falling asleep in bed with my girl in my arms. It makes me feel like I'm protecting her, and it makes her feel protected too. This helps both parties get the best night's sleep possible.

Of course, someone's arm or leg might fall asleep or even start to lose circulation. There's no ideal cuddling position. Both of you are going to have to maneuver and make the necessary adjustments throughout the night to maintain comfort. It might take a few attempts, but as you and she develop chemistry over time, you'll discover what works best. Before you know it, you'll both be making adjustments literally in your sleep, and then waking up in each other's arms. For guys who aren't "sleep cuddlers," I still strongly suggest that you at least hold her until she falls asleep, or until one of your limbs does -- then you are free to roll over and to catch some zzz's.

Oh, one more note while we're on the topic of middle-of-the-night displays of affection. If you're horny, there could be an opportunity for sex. Guys, there's nothing wrong with waking your girl up for some late night lovin', but please only pursue this when you know she doesn't have to be up early in the morning. Provided you're not in the doghouse, your girl might be up for this.

* * *

Here are more pointers on how to interact with your girlfriend: if possible, text (or instant message) her at least once, if not twice, a day. Keep it short and simple. In addition to being a couple, you still have your own lives and are busy with work and other responsibilities. "Hope you're having a good day, just thinking of you xoxo." This is something super simple that is good, no matter what state of mind she's in.

To give a more specific example, say you were watching TV together, and a funny line was said during a show or movie. You both burst into laughter and repeat the line for ten minutes straight. Text what it was that you two laughed about, or something related to it. Don't hesitate to be a little risqué with it either. If the two of you caught Adam Sandler in the cinematic classic "Billy Madison," go ahead and text her, "Nudie Magazine Day!"

If you shared a laugh about it the previous night, the next-day text is a cute gesture and will make her smile. This probably goes without saying, but your text doesn't have to be something like "Nudie Magazine Day!" All you want to do is pick something cute, funny, and specific to your relationship. Perhaps it's just "one of those days" for her; you can brighten it up by sending short, sweet messages. Make her feel loved. Show her that you are thinking about her.

Regarding texting and instant messaging, you'll want to continue to take advantage of other forms of communication and use the latest trends in technology to your benefit when reaching out. If neither of you use an instant messaging program, that doesn't mean that you can't contact her on the computer. Drop her a quick email or send her a Facebook message. Just let her know that you're thinking of her, without being overwhelming. You can even "poke" her (it's about the only thing poking is useful for).

There are other strategies that I suggest you use on Facebook. For instance, I urge you to change your relationship status to "In a relationship," and say whom it's with. Not everybody is going to be completely comfortable with announcing his or her relationship to the world, but let her make that decision, or make it together. Make it clear that you are proud to be with her, and you aren't ashamed about sharing this online.

That said, your relationship status changes do not have to appear in everyone's newsfeeds. Most people don't want hundreds, if not thousands, of people to see "Bob Smith has gone from 'in a relationship' to 'single'." Next thing you know, Bob is getting all sorts of comments and questions asking, "What happened?" There's a good chance that Bob's ex is still Facebook friends with him too. Avoid this awkwardness by going into your privacy settings. You can customize who's able to see what on your profile. Not everyone needs to know that you've been dumped or that you're with somebody new. Being aware of what your privacy settings are can keep your personal life a bit more private.

One more thing you can do on Facebook or Twitter (or whatever you use) is to change your default photograph to a shot showing the two of you together. Keep in mind, this isn't necessary, and it probably isn't even something you want to do early in a relationship. It's just another nice gesture to make her feel more secure, loved, and that further demonstrates that you're into her -- and not afraid to let others know. If the photos of the two of you are starting to accumulate, give her an album. Go ahead and title it "Me and my baby" or "My love," or whatever you're comfortable with.

Even though the online world plays a huge role in our daily lives, we shouldn't forget that real life matters most. It's not worth obsessing about relationship statuses and photo galleries. None of it matters in the long run. If you want to change your status, fine. Don't change it for public attention or any other misguided motives. Do it for her, and because you really want to. Remember, it's only Facebook. If the two of you are happy in the non-Internet real world, then who cares about anything else?

Take advantage of websites out there like e-cards.com. Send her an e-greeting card for no apparent reason. You're going to do more for her birthday anyway. If all you do for your girl on her birthday is send her an e-card, your relationship is going to be in lots of trouble. Be creative and be funny. Use cheesiness, but sparingly. Too much cheese is bad, but girls will respect you more knowing that it's coming from a good place. All the card has to do is convey something pleasant and perhaps make a reference to something that the two of you shared. It's the thought that counts!

We've talked throughout this book about different types of communication. We've analyzed calling, texting, and using the Internet to your advantage. The way I see it, there are three levels of communication: a) the time spent with her, b) talking on the phone, and, c) just about anything else that involves a computer or typing (texting, instant messaging, Facebook). Skyping (video chatting) can also be a useful form of communication. Your sarcasm isn't lost because you're able to see the other person's facial expressions and reactions. The digital era continues to evolve, as is the nature of how people in a relationship communicate with one another.

I'm quite aware that it's the 21st century, and people travel, often for work. Trips out of town can last a week or longer. In addition to phone and Internet communication, it's not a bad idea to send her a postcard or written letter when you're away. She'll be touched by your effort and old-school charm. As outdated as "snail mail" might seem, everybody still loves to get mail that isn't a bill or credit card offer. Even if she gets your postcard two days after you get back, she'll laugh and appreciate your kind gesture. The key is to take advantage of these different methods, but never neglect calling her on the phone and other traditional means of communication. Healthy relationships cannot survive exclusively on texting!

I also suggest that you keep a scrapbook or collection of souvenirs from your relationship. Save movie ticket stubs, matches, or business cards from the places where you've been together. Save the greeting cards she's given you for anniversaries or birthdays, the thank you notes and cards. Save that champagne bottle cork from New Year's Eve, or from that night you celebrated another special occasion.

When collecting items, try not to be obvious, as if you're some sort of weird packrat. Don't say, "Babe, pass me the wine cork," and then bizarrely stuff it into your pocket. Ideally, this should all be done on the down low. By amassing a collection of relationship artifacts, you can use these items to your benefit down the road. As early as three or four months into your relationship, you pull out your stash of goodies. By saving souvenirs, you're showing her that the times you've shared with her are important to you, and that the experiences have real meaning. In addition to giving her some of these random items as gifts, you may have a "get out of jail free card" on your hands. Even though you may have screwed up, you can try to use these items to trigger her memory of a happier past moment. Make it harder for her to stay mad at you. I wouldn't suggest giving your girlfriend an old movie ticket stub as a birthday or Valentine's Day present, but consider giving her a part of the stuff you've saved -- in addition to a real present.

While we're on the subject of gifts, it is essential to remember important dates like birthdays, anniversaries and Valentine's Day, February 14th. I understand that preparing for these special occasions can be challenging and even stressful.

For instance, I once dated a girl who had a birthday on January 23rd. This may seem like a harmless date for a girl to be born on, but think about the timing. Less than a month ago it was Christmas and New Year's, and Valentine's Day is just around the corner. When dates of special occasions are bunched on the calendar, it can put a strain not only on your mind, but also on your bank account. Love shouldn't be about money. An understanding girl will appreciate that it is the thought that counts, and not the monetary value of the presents you give.

The key is to prioritize. If you just bought her a designer purse or some sparkling bling for her birthday in January or February, it's not the end of the world if you don't go all out for Valentine's Day. If you're in a situation where money's tight, it doesn't mean you can't give her a romantic, memorable Valentine's Day.

If you've been paying enough attention to your girl, as I've been urging you to do all along, you'd know by now what her favorite food is. Make the effort and prepare a romantic dinner, something that she will really love. If some research is required, take advantage of your available resources, whether it is a family member who's skilled in the kitchen or a recipe on the Internet.

Assuming that you don't poison her, it's your effort that she'll applaud. Also, it doesn't hurt to make it a little more romantic atmosphere with a few tea candles around the table and the room (the little round ones in the tins that come in bags of 25 or so).

Items at a Formal Meal

1. Napkin	4. Service Plate	8. Seafood Cocktail Fork	12. Dessert Fork
2. Dinner Fork	5. Dinner Knife	9. Butter Spreader	13. Water Goblet
3. Salad Fork	6. Teaspon	10. Butter Plate	14. Wine Goblet
	7. Soup Spoon	11. Dessert Spoon	

Now, we've talked a bit about what to do if you're not skilled in the kitchen. It's fine to order in food on Valentine's Day, but remember, it's Valentine's Day. You should go beyond what might be a romantic dinner on any other night of the year. Even if you are going to cook her a meal from scratch, I strongly urge you to go the extra mile in other ways. On Valentine's Day, I suggest that you set up your place with extra flowers and candles. Have your iTunes playlist queued up with her favorite songs, and songs you both love. Even ask the florist for a basket of rose petals, and lay a path in your place. The rose petals can lead from the entryway to your bed -- and if you'd like, form heart shape on the bed itself. You also can create a path of rose petals that leads into your bathroom and bathtub. Put some petals around the tub too. Candles in the bathroom are also a must! If you want, fill up the bathtub with some water, just enough so that the rose petals and lit tea candles float, if you want to include those too.

If you recently exhausted funds on something special for her, a candlelight dinner can definitely suffice -- as long as she sees that you put in the thought, time, and energy that a good boyfriend should. Another thoughtful gift that you can give to your girl is a full body massage, significantly longer than the five- to ten-minute one described earlier. If you want to go all out, make dinner, then follow that up by giving her a soothing massage. After all this effort on your part, more than likely you will be rewarded…use your imagination.

Another tip to show your woman that she is special involves modern attentiveness. Almost everyone has his or her own smart phone, and most of them have a calendar or a notepad. Utilize this function to record data. When you guys are out together and she admires something in a storefront window, note this on your phone. If you guys are strolling through a mall or marketplace, pay close attention to the items that she shows interest in, tries out, or tries on. After a girl tries on clothes that she likes but decides not to purchase, often I'll rip the tag off and save it. This helps me in several ways: not only do I now know her exact size, I will now be able to head back to the store to locate the same outfit.

As you observe your girl's likes, note the name of the place, the item, or perhaps even grab a business card or flyer without her seeing you do this. The idea is to obtain enough information to help you later. Nothing is more thrilling than surprising your girl with something she actually wants, but would never expect you to remember. The real thrill isn't even so much in the actual gift; it's more that she'll be touched by your attention to detail, and that you actually took the time to listen to what she said. In addition to noting in your phone what your girl might like for her birthday, it goes without saying that you should remember her birth date. Use your phone to remember all important dates!

Naturally, your gestures will get more extravagant with time, so don't be in a rush to take her on vacations early in the relationship, even if you can afford it. Don't buy her expensive jewelry after only knowing her a few weeks, or even a couple of months. Use discretion with the money you spend on girls. A sad truth is that being in a relationship with a woman can become costly. Ask yourself if you're being smart and generous, or overzealous and wasteful, and somehow trying to buy her love. Over time, the expensive jewelry and clothing, the trips and vacations will come. I urge you to go at a comfortable pace and spend accordingly. If you set the bar too high too early, you could shoot yourself in the foot later when trying to live up to the unreasonable expectations that you've set.

It's important to remember the fun little touches to keep the relationship not only afloat, but happy, too. I know I sound like a broken record, but consistent complimenting is essential. Don't forget to do this, especially for the tasks that she's put effort into, such as makeup when she's getting ready to go out. Much of this is review, but remember -- don't compliment everything about her. If you over-compliment, what you're saying loses some of its value and overall oomph. Keep it simple. "You look beautiful. I love that outfit on you." The key is to be genuine. Look at her in the moment and compliment her on something relevant. Usually, complimenting nails is a good idea, unless much of the polish has faded and some nails are damaged. Don't just blurt out, "I like your nails." Look at her closely and be observant. Don't always give unspecific, generic compliments to her.

Give your compliments substance by not saying kind words for the sake of saying them. Not that you're on any sort of schedule, but as I've mentioned, it's always good to spread out your compliments and avoid rapid fire ones. Whether it's over the course of an evening, or over the course of a long-term relationship, consistency should be your goal. Complimenting can be another opportunity for you to keep things fresh by keeping her on her toes. It's those spontaneous moments, and comments you make, that will keep her smiling and the positive energy flowing.

* * *

It's time now to talk about how you really feel about your girl. Guys, there is no timeframe -- not a month, not three months, or even a year for that matter, for how long you should wait until saying those three little words. You'll know, and you'll feel it.

You now have undeniably strong feelings for this girl. You can't get her out of your mind. You're constantly thinking about her. You've let your guard down at this point, and in many ways you have become quite vulnerable. This is okay; these feelings are normal. There's no reason to be afraid of them, so enjoy and embrace them.

You all know which three words I'm referring to, and I hope that you will find the perfect moment to say, "I love you" out loud for the first time to her. Whether you like it or not, this is an important milestone in a relationship. Not to sound too dramatic, but you have reached a point of no return. After you say these special words, certain thoughts will run through your girl's mind. The best-case scenario is obviously her emphatically and quickly responding with "I love you, too."

After "I love you," the stakes are raised. It hits you hard and makes you realize the serious direction to which you've suddenly committed. Whether you're ready for it or not, you and she are inescapably going to view yourselves, each other, and your relationship in a new light. From this point on, it is sort of implied, if not expected, that you will be telling each other that you love one another on a regular basis. For example, when saying good night or good-bye, this is a nice time to remind your girl that you love her, by telling her just that.

You must remember that her thoughts will become serious now that "I love you" is out of the bag. It's no longer unreasonable for her to think of moving forward -- moving in with you, an engagement, or even a lifetime commitment together. "I love you" automatically raises the bar. I strongly advise that you allow enough time to let milestones come naturally, and not force out these powerful words. As frightening as this might sound to some guys, trust your instincts. Of course, merely saying "I love you" to a girl doesn't necessarily mean that you want a lifetime commitment with her just yet, either. All I'm saying is that if you feel it, say it, and if you don't feel it, don't say it. Don't let the pressures of a relationship force you into saying something you aren't ready to express.

So what do you do if you say "I love you" to a girl and she doesn't respond saying it back? There are a few different responses she could give: a smile, her telling you how sweet you are, a big hug and kiss -- but still not "I love you." If you get a response like this, it doesn't mean that it's over. She's still giving you a warm, positive response, but maybe she isn't where you are in the relationship yet. This is normal. Relationships are challenging, and it's impossible to be on the same wavelength as another human being all the time.

This scene can be quite tricky, and you'll have to figure this one out on your own. She will likely give you an explanation for her response (or lack of one). If you aren't satisfied with her explanation, remember, it might not be in your best interest to push her for reasons.

Every situation is unique, but it's always important to communicate. To be fair to yourself, it's reasonable to ask, "Are we moving forward here?" A day or a few days later (if not sooner) might be an ideal time to follow up with her if you're having doubts about her lack of a response to "I love you." If there's something troubling you, bring it up. Communicate!

If she says that she needs more time to sort things out, give her this time. Don't force the issue by trying to coerce her for answers right away, when she clearly isn't ready to respond to you. This can only make things worse. Tell her that you'd appreciate an explanation when she's ready to give you one, and that you're willing to be patient because she's important to you. Be reasonable, but also help her understand where you're coming from. If her response to the "I love you" talk is "I'm just not ready to say that yet," don't force the issue by making her say something that she doesn't mean. Don't freak out if she tells you that she "isn't there yet." If you hound her to tell you that she loves you back, do you really think she is going to mean it when she says it?

There are still other possible responses that people can have to being told "I love you." It's pointless for me to even begin to articulate all of them. I will tell you this, though. We all feel hurt when we put ourselves out there, only to be left hanging out to dry. Nobody enjoys being so vulnerable and risking so much. We are all dealing with the same concerns. We then start to question the relationship and ask ourselves, "If she can't love me now, could this girl ever really love me?"

After such a disappointing exchange, your mind might start to play tricks on you. Suddenly, you'll start thinking that she doesn't seem to be as interested in you as she once was. Your mind will start racing, and you'll start doubting yourself, perhaps even wondering if there could be another guy in the picture. Try to avoid such negative, paranoid thoughts. Remember that even if she didn't say "I love you" back, has anything else in your relationship really changed?

Maybe it seems like she's not calling or texting as much, and not showing the same amount of affection that she used to. Be careful: this could definitely all be in your head. Don't assume that she's not feeling as connected with you anymore. As we've discussed, if something is worrying you, talk about it with your girl, but please don't go overboard and come across as an insecure, overly sensitive guy. Being a whining, complaining baby is not something that your girl is going to find attractive.

For some people, saying "I love you" is nearly impossible, for others it comes out naturally. Now, what if you're a guy who's never really said, "I love you" before to anyone, let alone to someone with whom you've been romantic and intimate? What if you're shy, or come from an upbringing in which "I love you" was rarely spoken? When growing up in cold, seemingly loveless, repressed and unexpressive environments, it's no wonder that some guys are unable to express even basic feelings.

I do have advice for guys like this, but in no way, shape or form am I an expert on the psychology of the human mind and how it deals with emotions (or lack thereof). As I said in regards to topics related to diet, fitness, and even STD's, I strongly urge you to follow up with professionals. The same concept applies when it comes to your mental well-being. I want to make it clear that I'm very much in favor of anyone talking to a professional, if he or she chooses to. Whether it's a therapist, counselor, psychologist, or psychiatrist, these people are trained professionals that are here to help us.

This probably goes without saying, but not everyone who sees a professional therapist is crazy. Guys, you shouldn't feel like less of a man if you're in therapy. In fact, counseling, or even couples therapy can help make a relationship stronger. Whether you're in a relationship or not, please don't feel embarrassed or uncomfortable about getting help. Remember, nobody needs to know, and everything can be kept private and confidential. It seems like today, couples therapy is no longer just for Mom and Dad. Couples of all ages are taking advantage of the available resources -- ones that can help a relationship get through tough times. Whether it's an inability to say "I love you" or any other troubling issue, know that there are people out there who can help.

Moving on, nine times out of ten, your girl is waiting patiently for you to initiate and say those three words first. As difficult as this might be to swallow, you must dig deep, step up, and be the man in the relationship. Of course, it's going to be an intense moment when you tell a girl you love her for the first time. You're nervous, and maybe even afraid to blurt out this beautiful phrase. As ridiculous as this might sound, it's not a bad idea to practice saying, "I love you" in your bathroom mirror. Go ahead, try it. Maintain eye contact with yourself, and say these words with confidence and meaning behind them. This should be coming from your heart!

There's a very good chance that it'll be a little bit of an awkward moment when you do finally say "I love you" to your girl. Actually, it's kind of a "good awkward." Despite whatever awkwardness the two of you may be feeling, it will still be a beautiful, memorable moment. Have faith in yourself. Have the balls and confidence. Go ahead and blurt out, "I love you" -- preferably at an appropriate moment. If you're more comfortable planning this type of pronouncement in advance, set up a romantic evening or weekend together. Then tell her "I love you" when the timing is right. Trust yourself that you'll be able to recognize such a moment.

If you don't think that's your style, there's nothing wrong with being more spontaneous. A perfect romantic weekend is not always necessary. Say you're walking on the beach with your girl around dusk. Since you're holding hands already, now is a good time to glance over at her for a moment. Once again, realize how beautiful she looks in the rays of the sun. As your heart skips a beat, think to yourself, "Wow. That's mine. How lucky am I?" Try imagining your life without her. It's a gut-wrenching feeling. It's like someone punched you in the stomach and knocked the wind out of you. Appreciate what you have. If she says "I love you" back, then immediately kiss her. Follow it up by telling her something sweet about how grateful you are to have her in your life and how happy she makes you feel.

If the feelings I've just described were something that you can relate to, now would be an opportune time to tell your woman that you love her. There are countless ways to tell a girl that you love her for the first time. If deep down you know that you want to say, "I love you," but don't know how, all I can suggest is to go ahead and take that giant step by whatever means possible. As Nike would say, "Just do it." Make sure that she has your undivided attention, and that the environment is comfortable. For obvious reasons, you probably don't want to blurt out "I love you" to your girl for the first time in a crowded and loud social setting!

So, what do you do if your girl is the first person to blurt out "I love you"? This isn't necessarily a red flag, but it could be -- particularly if it's very early in the relationship. This goes both ways. Guys, be aware that if you prematurely tell a girl that you love her, she might be taken aback. Every relationship is different, and there is no correct timeline when deciding when to say "I love you" for the first time.

I believe that it's a man's duty to lead the way in a relationship. I don't mean to come across as chauvinistic, and I do realize that this is the 21st century, but certain old-school ideals (should) carry weight in today's world. The guy should be the one who takes charge by making the decision to push forward in a relationship. Now, before you girls get all bent out of shape, try to follow me here. At least 99 percent of the time, the guy is expected to be the one who gets down on one knee to propose. The guy is supposed to be the one to approach the girl's parents and seek their blessing before he proposes. Saying "I love you" is sort of a proposal to get to that next level in your relationship, but instead of her saying "Yes," you just want her to say, "I love you" back.

If you're caught completely off guard by her "I love you," and not ready to go to the next level, do not tell her you love her, too, just to tell her what she wants to hear. This will cause more problems in the long run. As hard as this might sound, you're better off being honest and upfront. Tell her, "I have very strong feelings for you. I care about you deeply." If that's how you really feel, you can say something like, "I'm very happy with how things are now, and where they seem to be going. However, I want to say what you want to hear when I'm ready."

That's pretty much all you can do if you find yourself in this situation. Most likely, your girl is going to feel hurt, and she might even lash out at you in anger. Even so, you're better off dealing with the immediate aftermath and moving on the best you can, rather than deceiving her by giving in and telling her that you love her when you don't (just yet). The bottom line is that lies and deception only delay inevitable problems, and can destroy a relationship.

A side note for you girls who might be reading this: please stop repeating yourself when it comes to the subject of marriage. Trust me, we heard you the first time. We pick up on your hints when you're putting them out there. Although we may appear to be so at times, we're not complete idiots, you know. When a girl talks about how beautiful a wedding she attended was (or what she'd do differently at her own wedding) we are well aware that marriage is something that she wants in life. We get it. When girls talk about how magnificent their friend's engagement ring is, or even say to their boyfriends, "We'd have the cutest kids together," we know what all of that means.

There's nothing wrong with being open about your wants and needs, but it is harping on the subject of marriage that does the opposite of the desired effect -- it pushes us away. Even if you're not using the "M word" on a regular basis, overwhelming us with obvious hints can be just as irritating, and it might actually prolong the time until the engagement day.

At the same time, guys must understand that as women age, their biological clocks are ticking -- and seemingly faster with each passing year, especially after they hit 30. Women are born with all the eggs they are ever going to have, and they don't make any new eggs during their lifetime. You should be aware that the average woman begins to become infertile by age 37.

While guys should be aware of this fact of nature, don't let this or anything else pressure you into a commitment you don't want or aren't ready for. Guys need to pay attention to the inner-workings of the minds and bodies of females, and much more so than we have been.

For girls, try to keep the marriage talk to a minimum, or at least be reasonable and not obsessive about it. Context matters, because it's one thing for a girl to be dating a guy for several years and wanting marriage, and the guy is just stalling -- and it's another story if a couple has been together for a few months and the girl mentions marriage every other day. Girls, all I'm saying is that marriage is something we know that you probably want!

* * *

Let's move on to some relationship problems. When in the midst of a serious relationship, do not hold things in and let them build up inside of you. The more you hold back, the more likely issues will fester and lead to a blowup. You want to avoid major fights the best you can, and you also want to avoid saying something you will regret. Think before speaking. I know this can be difficult, but if you say the wrong thing and it strikes a sensitive nerve, the damage could be irreversible. The same goes for her, too. We've talked briefly about this topic already, but I can't stress enough the importance of communication. In fact, it might be the most important element in a relationship. You'll want to be able to give each other critical feedback and be open about each of your concerns, whether it's a minor, annoying pet peeve, or a major problem. Feelings could be hurt here, but keep in mind that the strategy is to nip the issue in the bud and heal the wound before it grows and later scars.

Remember that focusing on the negative qualities of your mate will get you nowhere fast. You don't want to have these discussions regularly. The key is to remember how important it is to have such talks, at least once in a while, or on an as-needed basis. If there is an issue, talk it out within a day or two. Don't let concerns build up inside. But remember, if either you or she continue to criticize the other regularly, this will quickly become a toxic situation.

Often it's healthy not to over-analyze your

relationship. Why spend too much time focusing on trying to fix problems that may not even be fixable? Sometimes people are just who they are and can't be changed (we'll talk more about this in the next chapter). For the most part, it's more efficient to stay positive and embrace simple thoughts like, "I can't wait to see this girl again." Don't forget what attracted you to her in the first place, and what it is that you love about her. Ask yourself if you still feel committed and feel the passion for the person you are with. If the answer is yes and it's the same for her, hang in there, because there's a great chance that you guys can make it work. Just because you're angry right now, don't let the emotion you're feeling sway your long-term feelings about her.

This goes without saying, but answering these questions about feelings aren't always the easiest questions to answer, but they are ones that you need to be asking yourself, especially when your relationship is having trouble. It's important to also ask yourself, "Is it still a realistic possibility that I could be with this person for life, or is that possibility really out of the question at this point?"

Along with communication, another very important element of a relationship is trust. The two go hand in hand. If you and your girl don't communicate, trust will disintegrate. Keep the lines of communication as open as possible. Pick and choose your battles by deciding on times to address your concerns. This goes for both parties. It all depends on you, her, and the situation. Just because you're upset about something doesn't mean that you have to address these issues the second you see her.

One last item before I wrap up this chapter is that I

want to say again that relationships are challenging, but they can also be very rewarding. I just discussed the importance of sharing negative feedback, but in any healthy relationship, positive vibes should be most prominent. This is probably the hundredth time I've mentioned this, but never forget the value of complimenting. Remember, it's those special, spontaneous moments shared that help build a long-lasting, strong relationship.

I believe that even more important than your words are the actions that you take, but most females want it all. They want you to say the right things and do the right things too. In addition to communicating on a basic level, you must also find a way to express your feelings to her. Most guys consider feelings as foreign concepts, but unfortunately for us, girls value feelings and emotions deeply. They want to see you as a man's man and someone who is assertive, but also as someone who has a soft side and is able to express real feelings in a romantic way. Women want to have their cake and eat it too. And they will!

Chapter 14: Breakups, Moving On, & Final Words of Encouragement

One of the risks when entering a relationship is feeling open and vulnerable. There's always the strong possibility for heartbreak. You may not always feel like you are in control, but be confident in yourself, and over time you will discover what you want. That said, you have to learn to be both cautious and resilient when it comes to matters of the heart. No relationship is a straight road. There will be peaks and valleys -- problems and fights to overcome and get through. Not everything in a relationship is black and white. There are many gray areas, where you and your partner will have to be flexible. This concept is one of the keys to maintaining a healthy, successful, and balanced relationship.

Ideally, no partner should bend more than the other, but in actuality, this doesn't happen. I think guys should be willing to bend more, but as long as one person in the relationship isn't walked over and there's a semblance of balance, then the relationship has the potential to flourish. If there's prevailing unhappiness in the relationship or a lack of sparks present, do yourself a favor and seriously consider breaking it off before one person gets even more emotionally attached, and sets him or herself up for disappointment and heartbreak.

* * *

The following is not an unfamiliar scenario for most people: the relationship went full speed from the get go. It was love at first sight, as if I was in a romantic Hollywood movie. Nikki was beautiful, smart, talented, and driven. She was my perfect blond-haired, blue-eyed petite beauty, whom I'd been fantasizing about since I was in grade school.

We had countless first time moments as a couple, and when I would wake up in the morning and look over at her, I'd think to myself, "Wow. I can't believe how lucky I am to be with such a beautiful girl." More importantly, she was full of surprises, and she always made me laugh, learn, but most importantly, feel loved. Things clicked for us, and I never enjoyed the simple moments in life as much as I did with her. Whether we were sharing a Sunday morning breakfast together, hiking in the Santa Monica Mountains or cuddling on the couch in the evening, I felt at peace with myself, with her, and with the world around me. I found joy in daily tasks like food shopping or doing laundry, so long as Nikki was by my side. I've always considered myself the type to get married, but with Nikki, for the first time, I seriously thought about such a future.

Things didn't immediately start to go sour, but slowly over time, little things about her started to get to me more and more. When you're in the midst of a relationship that's clearly struggling, you and your girl might both be oblivious to certain problems, issues that people around you can easily see. It's hard to let go when you and she are both so determined to make it work. You both are being stubborn, but it's unhealthy to live in denial. In your heart, you might believe that you're really right for her and that she is right for you, but reality proves otherwise. Just like many of you out there, I, too, have lived through this.

With Nikki, the same issues kept surfacing, getting progressively worse over time. The fights were more intense and frequent. Early on in the relationship there were quarrels, but we thought we had squashed the issues and moved past them. I really believed in my heart that we moved past the "make it or break it" conflicts. By "make it or break it," I'm referring to either being able to move past the issues, or deciding that the problems cannot be worked out and the relationship has to end. I honestly thought that we had worked through most of our major issues.

Despite the great make-up sex that always seemed to follow our quarrels, soon enough, certain unfortunate patterns kept repeating. There's a fine line between a fight that is plain stupid, and another that will become a continuous problem that creeps back into your relationship. Listen people: stupid fights are stupid fights, but some issues are cancerous, real threats to the happiness and longevity of your relationship.

The key is to be able to identify red flags early. What are you willing to tolerate and compromise on in this relationship? If you don't see yourself being able to live with certain personality quirks or behaviors, remember that this is who she is. People are all imperfect. All we can do is pick and choose our battles with our lovers. Are you willing to love her and overlook certain vices? Are you hopeful that certain issues can be resolved over time? Are you blindly hoping that she's going to change just for you? The thing is, you might be able to recognize a girl's shortcomings, but to some degree, that just might be who she is. Most people don't actively want to hurt the person they're in love with, and people don't always have control over who they are.

Whether it's due to your parents' influence, past relationships, or any other contributing factors people are sometimes unaware of their own behaviors and the damage they cause.

On the flip side of the coin, she's asking herself the same questions. You know that she has her own views on everything, which will often differ greatly from what you believe to be the truth. Consider how hard it is for you to change, and you'll quickly understand what little chance you have in trying to change others. Take that in for a second or two, because there's a meaningful life lesson there, and it's something I had to learn the hard way.

Nikki will always be a special girl and have a piece of my heart. Not that I'm a saint by any means, but I realized that her faults were irreversible, and they only became more prominent over time. I'm not perfect, and I have my own issues, but Nikki was plagued with mistrust and insecurities, a devastating combination. She claimed that she had never had trust issues in the past because in her previous relationships, she was always in total control. I never gave her a single reason to not trust me, but I wasn't going to let her walk all over me as she had done with other guys.

Every time I wasn't with her, Nikki was suspicious of my whereabouts, despite me always being in contact with her via text or phone call. Many people have some insecurity issues when they're in relationships, but this girl took it to a whole new level. She was paranoid that I didn't feel what she felt about us, and no matter what I said to her, did for her, or even bought for her, nothing seemed to put her mind at ease.

I was so far in love and invested in this girl that I

started to neglect other people in my life. When in a serious relationship, a person tends to spend the majority of his or her free time with the significant other, but I was so intent on spending as much of my free time with Nikki, that I slowly, unknowingly pushed away genuine friends. I spent more and more time with her the longer we dated, and less time with others.

Everyone makes compromises when they're in a serious relationship. There are only so many hours in a day, and unfortunately, you can't be everywhere at once. It can become challenging to find the time to please everyone in your life. In a relationship, you're going to spend more and more quality time with your girlfriend and less time with your friends, yet you should always try your best to keep the lines of communication open with your friends. If you truly value their friendships, prioritize your life to make time to see them. If you're genuinely making the effort, they'll understand and be willing to make compromises too. After all, a lot of them are going to be in and out of relationships and dealing with the same dilemmas as you. True friends are people who understand, are able to compromise, and want nothing more than to see each other find love and be happy. I never thought of myself as someone who shut friends out. I never thought I'd become that person.

But one day, Nikki was out of town, and I woke up and realized that I was suddenly in need of a ride to the airport. The few reliable people that I'd usually call were unavailable, so I had to consider other friends. These were people who I liked and considered to be good friends, but I quickly realized that I hadn't spoken to any of them in a while. I began to consider how awkward and even lame it would be to ask for such a favor from them;

at the time I hadn't been showing much interest in their friendships.

On the rare occasion that I was "allowed" out for a night with friends, Nikki never made me feel at ease. She never showed that she trusted me. I'd have drinks on a random weeknight with coworkers and arrive home a little later than normal, on evenings when we had no set plans. I would tell her where I was and that I would be home in a couple of hours. Immediately upon updating her over the phone, she would either give me the silent treatment or short, snappy answers. She wouldn't say overtly that she was upset, but I could tell by the tone of her voice and her "I don't care what you do" attitude that she was upset.

If I didn't get these passive-aggressive responses, the other type I got was overtly hostile. She'd go on about how I wanted my "single life," and how I preferred to be with my friends over her. She often interrogated me, and this became a repeating pattern. It became impossible for me to spend quality time with friends or coworkers without having to deal with repercussions and feeling unnecessary guilt, as if I'd done something terribly wrong.

Gradually, Nikki's behavior became more and more damaging to our relationship. I always thought of myself as an unselfish friend and boyfriend, and I have tried to put others before me, especially Nikki. Whether it was listening to her talk about her work politics or helping her fix something in her apartment, I always tried to be accommodating. However, sometimes I was unable to drop everything at a moment's notice and give Nikki the undivided attention she wanted.

I have other examples of things she said and did

that upset me, and ultimately destroyed me. One time it was the middle of a workday during a busy week when she called me. She told me that the garbage disposal side of her kitchen sink was clogged and that her sink was filled with murky water. I told her that I would stop by when I got off work to take a look. She asked me if I could take off a little early. I told her that I couldn't, and that's when she got upset and flew off the handle, "How can I count on you in life if you can't even do something this simple for me?!" I tried to give instructions over the phone and told her to just hit the reset button on her disposal, but she continued to shout over me and pleaded for me to come over right away. Since her sink wasn't even overflowing, I begged her to wait just a few more hours. She wouldn't listen, and of course, the conversation ended with her abruptly hanging up on me. Several angry texts came next. These kinds of incidents happened a bunch of times, and I'd respond calmly and lovingly, only to be ignored or responded to in a degrading, selfish manner -- making me out to be the worst boyfriend ever.

She made me feel like I could never please her enough. I felt that I could never make her happy or do the right thing. It came to a point where no matter how much I put her needs ahead of mine it was never enough. She ultimately pushed the idea out of my mind that she could be the one, when all I ever wanted was for her to realize how much I truly loved and cared for her, and our relationship.

As much as I tried to communicate to her what upset me, I eventually reached my breaking point and had to do one of the hardest things I've ever had to do in my life. It wasn't so much one thing she said or did that stuck out. The choice that I made came from the accumulation of the fights, tears, and sleepless nights I had throughout this relationship. I understand now more than ever that no relationship is perfect and that everybody has to deal with disagreements. It's sometimes healthy to "agree to disagree," but if there's a repeating pattern, what you're likely doing is sweeping the issues under the rug by not dealing with them head on. There is definitely a difference between agreeing to disagree from a healthy standpoint, as opposed to ignoring the same major issues that plague a relationship. Trust me, if important issues aren't dealt with in a timely manner, soon enough they will come to a boiling point and blow up in your face.

Breaking up with Nikki was one of the hardest decisions that I've ever had to make, especially because there were moments when I thought this might be the girl I'd get down on one knee for, and that we'd spend the rest of our lives together. In a state of heartbreak, I truly believe that ending the relationship was the best move for me. I reached my breaking point and was mentally, physically, and emotionally exhausted. I had no fight left, and I could not handle any more stressful fights and unhappiness that came from the relationship.

I can't put into words the chemistry we shared and the connection between us. I really loved her and treated her like a princess. I do realize what I lost, and I hope that she realizes what she lost too. Looking back, I learned a great deal about myself and what my needs are in a relationship; I now feel emotionally stronger. In addition, I truly hope that she gained wisdom from the experience that was our relationship, and someday she finds the happiness that she deserves.

I don't know how anyone can move on, and I can tell you right now that I don't know how the hell I did it myself. When you love someone so much, it's hard to restrain yourself from texting, calling, or trying to see the person again after you've broken up. I wish you the very best if you're going through something similar right now. I feel for you, but it's amazing how resilient we can be when circumstances are at their worst. Despite the agony caused by the breakup, we can still manage to keep productive by moving ahead with our lives as each day passes. What I do know is that the emotional stress will diminish over time. You'll miss your ex, and your heart will feel a little empty, but you'll learn to deal with this -- at least until the right person for you comes along.

It's normal and even healthy to throw out (or delete) stuff related to an ex. Go ahead. Be a little cold-hearted. Whether it's a photo on your mantle or computer, you have to be strong and get rid of it. If you can't bring yourself to throw out any of this stuff, at least store the items in a box that fits under your bed or in the back of your closet. It could be months (or even longer) before you start to get over her. Why make things harder on yourself by keeping reminders of your ex around in plain sight?

Someday, you might be able to view the contents of this box with a healthy perspective, by looking back and realizing that you made the right decision. Perhaps you'll be able to part ways with these items. There's no right or wrong way to handle this, as long as you're learning, moving forward, and maintaining a healthy outlook on your future dating life.

I know how crazy it is to love someone so much. As hard as it may seem to do in the moment, we must stay strong and move on with our lives. Remember that in the end, you'll start remembering the beginning. In being strong, you'll get to a place where you will remember and appreciate the happier times, while being fully aware of what plagued your relationship and brought it to an end. You'll be smarter and more confident. Through experience, there's always wisdom to be gained. Granted, it's not the most painless route to gaining wisdom, but through failure and missteps, you'll come to realize that even though it's another cliché, what doesn't kill you really does make you stronger.

* * *

Now you're probably asking yourself, "What do I do if I run into an ex?" Funny you should ask, because I actually ran into Nikki recently at Ralph's supermarket. Here's how it went down: it was a Sunday night and I was doing my usual grocery shopping for the week. I was strolling down the salad dressing and condiments aisle, and when I looked up, sure enough, there she was pushing her cart and coming toward me. When we finally made awkward eye contact, we both had that deer in the headlights look. I then gave her another quick look and was about to smile, but she quickly turned her cart around and headed in the other direction, immediately putting her cell phone to her ear.

What I want to convey is that although such awkwardness can reach painful lows, there's nothing wrong with acting like a stranger when bumping into an ex. It doesn't mean that you hate one another or that you're disrespecting the relationship that you guys shared. In these random situations, you don't owe a conversation to an ex. Nobody should feel obligated to make meaningless chitchat. In fact, it's probably best not to waste each other's time and energy in this spot. You broke up for a reason, and if the break-up happened recently, you might not be ready to communicate with your ex yet.

It doesn't always get easier. A couple of weeks later, guess who I ran into at the Tropicana Bar at the Roosevelt Hotel? Yup, that's right, and this time she wasn't alone. Nikki was with a guy, and it clearly was a date, evidenced by the fact that they were holding hands. I could see that she was leading him right in my direction. They were walking toward me, and this time she wasn't trying to avoid me. She seemed to be making a point that she was with a new guy. Although it's somewhat pointless for me to even speculate as to what her exact motives were, my guess would be that she was trying to go out of her way to show me that she had moved on. She may have wanted to make me feel a little jealous as well by reminding me what I gave up.

Guys, if you do happen to run into your ex and she's with a new guy, don't make a scene. Remember that he hasn't done anything wrong to you. There's no reason to start trouble.

As Nikki walked by me, our eyes locked. This time she stared back, acknowledging me with a half smile. No words were exchanged, but in return I gave her a half-smile too.

Back in the supermarket, she avoided any sort of interaction, but this time I could sense based on her eyes and how she was gazing at me that she missed me. When you know someone on a deep level, you pick up on their subtle idiosyncrasies that others overlook. In that moment, I believed that she still had feelings for me. I was able to sense how she was feeling, because I was experiencing something very similar. However, I knew that I had to be strong and continue on with my chin up. It was painful to see her in public with another guy, but in retrospect this actually helped me realize how important it was for me to move on. It sucks, but we have to keep moving forward. Keep in mind that a lot of what we're discussing here is advice that girls can take as well when it comes to handling the situation when you bump into an ex-boyfriend.

All situations vary, but the key is to be respectful. You do not want to argue with an ex in public and make a scene. At the same time, though, you want to hold your ground by coming off as a strong and confident person. Remember that the social setting you're in comes into play, and this will help dictate your actions. For example, should you run into an ex in a crowded public area, it's much easier to avoid an interaction. However, if you're in a place where only a small number of people are present and you run into an ex, you might have to grin and bear it. There's a very good chance that you'll have pretty much no choice but to have some unwanted, awkward conversation.

If you spot an ex while you're out with friends, you may have the option to leave the premises entirely, thus avoiding any potential awkwardness or drama. If leaving is an option for you and is your preferred choice, I fully support this decision. If you leave a place where your ex is, you shouldn't feel like she's "winning" or that you're at a lower level than her. There's no reason for you to have second thoughts. In fact, you're actually being mature by making a decision that's best for you, her, and the friends you're out with. Assuming this is a regular weekend night with friends, if they are true friends they will understand your desire to head to a different place. One more thing: if you see her heading out first, then you win! Just kidding.

Moving on, I've shared a couple of examples of how to handle these types of situations, but there's many more ways to handle yourself, depending on the particular situation. If you find yourself conversing with an ex you've run into, this is not something to lose sleep over. If you're the type who feels comfortable conversing with an ex, that's fine. However, if you know that keeping your distance from her is the healthiest thing to do, re-opening lines of communication could prove to be counterproductive to achieving closure and fully moving on. It's your call. There's no right or wrong answer, and it all depends on you, her, and where you guys are in your breakup. If the breakup was recent and bitter, you might choose one route. If you've been broken up for a while, you might decide to handle the interaction another way.

* * *

Sometimes we feel like we want a relationship to work out so badly that we can overlook some irreversible flaws in our ex, and we ill-advisedly get back together. There are many motives and factors for why a person might get back together with an ex for the wrong reasons, usually involving fear, such as: fear of being alone, afraid to start over, fear of being lonely during the holiday season, fear you won't find someone as attractive, or just the fear that you won't be into the next person as much as you were with your ex. Age can also become a factor, because people tend to settle on option B or C, when option A might still be out there.

Now, if you decide to get back together with an ex, understand that it's never going to be exactly the same that it was when things first were amazing between the two of you. There will be questions, concerns, and hesitations on both sides. Also, know that people aren't going to change overnight, if they can even change at all. If you and your ex do want to get back together, do it for the right reasons. I don't need to go into a long spiel that explains what the right and wrong reasons could be. That's between you and your girl. Just make sure that you do your homework and really think about it. Listen to your family, close friends, and people you trust. Most importantly, listen to your heart!

Everyone goes through break-ups, and when we're in the midst of one, we spend a considerable amount of time focusing on what didn't work, as well as the negative qualities in our ex. I'm here to tell you that there's no reason to always feel guilty about judging people. When you go out with a girl, you're judging her along the way -- and she, you. In romance, however, it's not whether the girl is perfect, but whether or not she is perfect for you.

I'm telling you that as time passes, you will reminisce more about memories of the good times that you and your girl once shared. There are very few things in life that are more rewarding than being in a happy, successful relationship. Many people share a popular viewpoint that almost all relationships are doomed to fail. In a country where the divorce rate remains high, it's no wonder that so many people submit to such a pessimistic outlook. If you approach your dating life with such a hopeless attitude, in a sense you're shooting yourself in the foot before the get go and not really giving yourself (and a new girl) a chance. I'm proud to say that this isn't me, and although we all have our moments of doubt and even despair, I don't allow such feelings to consume me -- and you shouldn't either!

Also, I'm not ashamed to say I believe that soulmates exist. If you feel that your significant other is your soulmate, then that person is. You can't prove that soulmates exist, but you can't disprove them either. If you claim someone is your perfect match and true soulmate, who's to question it? Experiencing such intense feelings about another person is a wonderful gift. Whether you believe in soulmates or not, what does it matter? All that matters is that you believe on a basic level that there is someone out there for you to love and grow old with.

What's most important is that we all try to put ourselves in positions that give us the best chance to find love and happiness in life. Who knows how to find happiness? It's the question that humanity has pondered for all time. Happiness is not something that is guaranteed in life. This is especially true because happiness means one thing to someone, but is defined differently by someone else. Much of what we've discussed doesn't come with guarantees, but it is more about giving you the best opportunity to find what it is that brings you closer to your soulmate, and that elusive happiness that we all seek. To quote Sir Paul McCartney, "The love you take is equal to the love you make." Spelled out, the more you put into life, the more you get out of it.

I can't stress enough my belief that there is someone out there for every single one of us. Don't give up. Even after dating and going through failed relationships, I'm still hopeful, and you should be too. There is hope because we see people in our families and lives that are in flourishing relationships. To some degree, all families are dysfunctional and have problems, but look at your parents, grandparents, and the married friends in your life. The married people you know can't all be miserable!

Take a moment and think about some of the married couples you know. Ask yourself, "Are these people I admire?" Like them, "Can I see myself someday going the distance as well? Do I hope to emulate their lifestyle?" To clarify, I'm not telling you to look at Ted and Susan Smith and copy their every move.

Of course, all couples have disagreements, but it's very important to learn to agree to disagree sometimes. Once again, agreeing to disagree is not the same as ignoring an issue by sweeping it under the rug. Agreeing to disagree is hearing your partner out, considering his/her point of view, and respecting it fully. At the same time, both parties can stand by what they believe. Couples who are unable to communicate well tend to sweep issues under the rug by ignoring the problems at hand. On the other hand, couples that reach a point where they can agree to disagree, may not always see eye to eye, but they still maintain productive dialogue with one another.

Again, in terms of taking a look at married couples in your life, there's nothing wrong with having a bit of an "If them, why not me?" mentality. For me, it's all about finding what I like to refer to as "the one," a.k.a. "my princess," to make the kingdom that I have built complete. This might not be something that you consciously know about, but sooner or later, most guys really do want to get married and have kids (or at least have someone to grow old with).

There comes a time when we all have to grow up and become men. Most of us will discover that our priorities evolve over time. What was important to you when you were 20 might not hold the same value when you're 25, 30, or 40 plus. Stability is something that comes with finding a career that is both challenging and financially rewarding. Whether we like it or not, women and children cost money. In other words, you must work extremely hard to support the ones you love. Romance requires passion, and so should everything you experience and strive to achieve in your life.

I'm not saying that the man works and the woman stays at home. Just as I've described, sharing the duties of cooking, cleaning, and laundry is essential. In today's world, it's often hard for couples and families to survive on a single income. In other words, if you as a man still hold onto the belief that a woman shouldn't work, I suggest that you abandon this notion immediately. This is especially true if you're with a girl who is not only qualified to be in the workforce, but one who also has a strong desire to pursue her own career. Even so, there's absolutely nothing wrong with a woman choosing to not work -- and that's whether she's raising a family or not. The key is that it should be her choice to not work, and this choice is something that you must be comfortable with, otherwise she's probably not right for you.

* * *

Love, trust, communication, security, and tolerance are important, but so is Windex-ing your countertops and opening the door for a woman. Let me put it this way: if you took in as little as ten percent of what this book has to offer, that's okay. As the writer, I'm still elated that you benefited by picking up a few useful pointers. It is my hope that a broad range of guys have found some of my ideas, thoughts, and opinions insightful.

While I did think about who my target audience might be, at the same time it was never really my true intention to seek out a specific demographic, other than guys searching for advice. I want girls to realize that some of us guys (as foolish as we may appear at times) really do take the time to pay attention to details, such as the amount of work that goes into your appearance -- the hair, the nails, the clothing, everything. For us guys, more or less, we just brush our teeth, shower, put on clothes, and then we're out the door. We should be more appreciative of the efforts (and sometimes countless hours) that females put into themselves.

Before I started writing this, I felt like I had a lot of answers and insight, but through the journey of writing this book, I've come to realize that there's a lot more for me to learn. I know that I don't have all the answers, and it would be foolish to claim that I do.

I hope that through reading this, you have enough information to go out into the world with a higher level of confidence and self-esteem. My most sincere wish is that every single one of you who has purchased *It's All About Her* found valuable information that you can apply in your everyday life.

Many of you guys have certain philosophies and routines that have worked well. I want you to pick and choose from my suggestions in order to improve in whichever aspects of life you decide. It's up to you. Hopefully by now, I have answered many questions that arise for us guys. Have I addressed some concerns that plagued you in the past? If so, do you see yourself in a new light now? I hope that you have picked up a few practical pointers that can help you out immediately.

It's not about molding you into me, or molding you into anybody else. My goal is to help give you the tools, determination, and courage to be the person you not only should be, but want to become. I don't want to change who you are, but merely bring to the surface the person you've always wanted to be, but for one reason or another haven't been able to become.

In Conclusion

If you've never had the opportunity to learn much about girls from your siblings, your parents, or other mentors in your life, I have something to tell you. Through this book, on some level, I want you to look at me as such a person in your life. Think of me as someone looking over shoulder, who has your back at all times, someone you can rely on at the end of the day. When questions come up relating to modern courtship, use me as a resource. I also want to offer guidance to help you get off to the right start and build more confidence in yourself. Even though I've been lucky to have two very loving big sisters, I've always wished for the opportunity to help out a younger brother.

With this book, it is my deepest and most sincere wish to reach as many guys as possible -- those who are looking for a friend with some answers. I feel honored that you've let me into your life through this book. When seeking genuine advice, nobody wants to be fed bullshit. I promise you that I am not the type who would do such a disservice to anyone who seeks guidance for his personal life.

I've shared constructive criticism. For example, how many times have I said the phrase, "Don't do this" or "Don't do that" when offering practical advice? Remember that you're not alone and it's okay to admit that you're flawed. Someone out there will love you despite your flaws. Be patient, and don't put too much pressure on yourself by always looking for love. It usually comes when you least expect it.

Personal growth never seems to happen overnight. It happens through years of trials and tribulations, whether that means too many one-night stands, short- and long-term relationships, or long-distance relationships. Everyone takes their own journey. I've come to realize a lot about who I am and what I want out of life. It takes a strong man to follow through and be committed to his ideals, and that's what you and I should be striving toward.

I know what type of girl I want to marry. I know the type of person I want to spend the rest of my life with. I know the kind of person I am, and what I deserve. There should be no reason why you shouldn't think the same way, especially after reading this book!

But in the end, it is my belief that you are who you are, and that no matter how hard people try to change each other, it never seems to work out. Nobody should compromise who he or she is as an individual. However, I hope that in some small way, I helped bring out the best in you -- your endearing traits that girls perhaps haven't even recognized...yet.

About the Authors

LANCE RANZER is a Visual Effects Artist and Supervisor for major motion pictures. Some of his credits include Oscar-winning films for Visual Effects: "The Curious Case of Benjamin Button" and "Hugo." Ranzer earned a Bachelor of Fine Arts degree from the University of Central Florida, majoring in Computer Animation with a Visual Effects & Compositing minor. When not working, he enjoys rock climbing, snowboarding, traveling to see ancient wonders of the world, and spending quality time with family and friends. Born in Brooklyn, NY, and raised in Orlando, FL, Ranzer currently resides in Los Angeles, CA -- a place that could always use more chivalry. Twitter: @allaboutherbook

ADAM CHOIT is a writer, producer, filmmaker, poet, and activist. Originally from Long Island, NY, he currently resides in Los Angeles, CA. He is a die-hard New York Mets fan and enjoys eating tuna melt sandwiches. Twitter: @adamjchoit